David Kauders

The Greatest Crash

How contradictory policies are sinking

the global economy

Sparkling Books

The Greatest Crash

List of figures

List of tables

Introduction

All round the world, many governments are in serious financial trouble. Many of them don't really understand why and have little idea what to do about it. Should governments try to reduce their annual deficits faster ... or more slowly? (Of course, few governments can hope to reduce their national debts for several years, unless they default.) Does the UK government's approach make more sense than the US government's? Surely they can't both be right?

It is perhaps too easy for armchair critics in the United Kingdom to take comfort in our decision not to join the Euro-zone. It is true that our exchange rate is not 'fixed' in the same way, but the British government's essential problem is not so very different from that of the governments of Greece, Ireland and Portugal.

Adam Smith said 'There's a deal of ruin in a nation', and it would be a mistake to despair. But one of the things we need now is new thinking on the fundamentals. That is what David Kauders provides in his book 'The Greatest Crash.' Most readers will learn a good deal from his provocative insights, even though few may agree with everything he writes. Warmly recommended.

Professor D. R. Myddelton,
Chairman of the Institute of Economic Affairs

Preface

Many human interest stories about the credit crunch have already appeared. Politicians have lined up their scapegoats, journalists have offered their opinions, economists have questioned their theories. There has been a substantial debate between those who believe austerity is now needed and those who argue for continued economic stimulus. This is the heart of the problem, since I believe both camps mean well but represent two sides of the same problem, namely a roadblock in the global financial system. Like a speed governor in a lorry engine, or a road junction that has no more traffic capacity, this system limit prevents further financial growth.

In researching this book, I found five previous books particularly useful in aiding my understanding of aspects of the change in the financial system. There are many others, but the reader who wishes to learn more should consult:

1. *Fantasy Island*, by Elliott and Atkinson,[1] which exposed Britain's enormous debt problem.

2. *The Black Swan*, by Nassim Nicholas Taleb[2] and *Lecturing Birds on Flying*, by Pablo Triana[3], which need to be read together. They debunk the statistical assumptions underlying derivatives trading. In doing so, they show the limits of much financial theory.

3. *Verdict on the Crash*, by a panel at the Institute of Economic Affairs[4], which identified the responsibility of governments in precipitating the crisis by creating asset bubbles. The contributors argue that more regulation is of little relevance.

4. *Fool's Gold*, by Gillian Tett[5], which records almost the entire history of how credit derivatives developed, showing how increasingly absurd assumptions were made about what derivatives could achieve, how they worked and the risks involved. Tett describes the devastating consequences of the entire episode as "a terrible, damning indictment of how twenty-first-century Western society works."

The ideas I develop in *The Greatest Crash* are unconventional. However, I hope to alert those willing to think broadly about the direction taken by global policy and start a debate about more useful alternatives to austerity versus stimulus. Above all, though, I hope to make the subject intelligible to everyone.

The need to challenge the status quo and develop a new conceptual framework underlies this book. To show why a new framework is needed, I ask you to consider the explanations that appear from official sources:

1. Bankers' bonuses are too high, encouraging banks to take bigger and bigger risks, thus endangering the financial system. Bonuses are asymmetrical, allowing banks to declare profits and pay bonuses in the good times, but leaving society at large to pick up the pieces in the bad times.
2. China's trade with the West has generated imbalances.
3. *The Economist* published an extensive analysis of what had gone wrong in summer 2009, and argued that finance and economics professionals needed to understand one another better.

Now contrast these with **my** main arguments:

1. The financial system cannot be expanded indefinitely.

2. People's financial behaviour has changed, and the change is irreversible, since borrowing is no longer desirable.

3. Economic relationships have changed and no longer follow the textbooks (see chapter 7).

4. Under pressure for regulatory conformity, society is losing the capability to adapt and learn.

5. Divided into compartments and overwhelmed with technical detail, few can now see the broad issues.

6. Many courses of action recommended by experts bring undesirable consequences.

I hope to elucidate the contrast and, in the final chapter, set out some ideas for the future.

Although most of my detailed examples refer to Britain, the points I make apply globally. Indeed, some of the problems that I highlight **are** global as a result of technical co-ordination through European and international standards and accepted practices.

As always with a work such as this, many others have contributed both directly and indirectly. I should particularly like to thank Sue Merron for the extensive help she has given me with the source material, challenging my arguments then knocking my erratic writing into shape. David Myddelton gave me considerable advice and encouraged the entire project. Frank Fishwick corrected my economics, George Hall commented on accounting practice and Elaine Turtle reviewed my opinions on pensions. Any remaining errors are entirely my own.

David Kauders
(a founder member of Kauders Portfolio Management AG)
Zug, Switzerland
October 2011

The Greatest Crash

How contradictory policies are sinking

the global economy

1 The roadblock preventing growth

The concept of a financial system limit

This book argues that it is impossible to expand the financial system much further. The financial system depends on debt and credit, which are equal and opposite. Borrowers acquire debt, financed by savers and intermediated through banks. In order to expand the financial system and therefore the global economy, it is necessary to find more borrowers, or for existing borrowers to borrow more, or a combination of the two.

For the moment I wish to put governments on one side and consider the private sector, from where all growth comes. The private sector consists of households, businesses and voluntary bodies. For this analysis, voluntary bodies are a subset of businesses, some with business-like activities, others with social purposes.

Households can barely afford their existing debts, let alone take on more. Since households now prefer not to borrow, indeed some even choose to pay back debt, it follows that those who have already borrowed, as a group, can no longer contribute to economic expansion.

People can be divided into borrowers and savers. With existing borrowers unable to afford or unwilling to take on extra debt, can new borrowers be found instead? Those who do not need to borrow are unlikely to volunteer. Except for the young wishing to buy houses, facing the reality that house prices are beyond their pockets, where are the new borrowers?

Businesses are also under pressure. There has been an inadequate

1

recovery from recession, business prospects are poor as households cut back their spending. Lack of bank lending is a symptom rather than a cause, for if existing businesses were to be given more credit, they would probably be unlikely to find profitable growth opportunities in a world of austerity.

Will enough new businesses emerge, financed by debt, to fill the void caused by lack of personal borrowers? No doubt there will be some, but the scale of their emergence and growth is likely to be inadequate. On the other side of the equation, existing businesses are failing with unpaid debts, causing banks to face losses and thereby cutting the availability of new credit.

This is the financial system limit: lack of new borrowing plus excessive weight of debt obligations from past borrowing combine to slow economies down. This is a barrier whichever way policy makers turn. It is like the lid on a boiling kettle. Enough steam can lift it for a while but it always snaps back into place. The financial system limit is a roadblock preventing growth[6].

Academics have already noted the limits to debt growth[7], yet governments prefer to continually expand credit in the belief that it is a useful economic policy. This either causes short-term retail price inflation or asset price inflation. Any retail price inflation resulting from credit expansion is transient, fading away in a year or two. Asset price inflation lasts longer but also fades when the next crisis appears[8]. Each economic stimulus is larger, costs more and has progressively less effect. The bill falls due, usually with each recession.

The cost of debt service eventually becomes the tail that wags the dog. As fewer people can afford to pay interest, demand for new loans falls and banks become choosier to whom they lend: supply also falls. As lending shrinks, economic activity stagnates, unemployment rises and the *existing* stock of debt becomes harder to service. Japan, Greece, Ireland and Portugal are in this trap, Britain is heading into it. I contend that the stagnation since the summer of 2007 arises directly from the impossibility of expanding the supply of credit any further.

It is likely that lost employment following this credit crunch will persist for years and therefore cause a worse rise in household arrears and repossessions (that is, defaults in the private sector) than has been known previously. Bad debts are already rising, unemployment is high, part-time work is replacing full-time work and therefore the capacity of households to service their existing debt will shrink.

Taxpayers cannot afford to reimburse unlimited losses, which constrains the extent to which governments can continue to provide bailouts. Both the Tea Party movement in the United States of America and German resistance to supporting the weaker Eurozone countries demonstrate this political limit, which I will expand on in chapter 5.

While the system limit I have identified is fundamental, systems thinking is also lacking. Systems thinking is the broad discipline of how things fit together and interrelate, as opposed to the narrow detail of measuring and controlling individual components of any activity. Systems thinking recognises that every system is part of a larger system, and therefore boundary assumptions merely serve to obscure the bigger picture. Systems thinking also recognises that classification schemes are arbitrary and serve to suppress characteristics that might give us insight into change. Such broad analysis could reduce the law of unintended

3

consequences, which arises whenever policy makers act without understanding the interrelationships between different elements in society.

One of my themes is that it is no longer possible to have your cake and eat it while paying nothing for it. The era of the Internet has brought price comparison shopping, while the era of the discounter has brought cheap no-frills services. Airline tickets, consumer goods of all types, intangibles such as insurance, even books, have all seen price deflation as discounting has spread. In parallel, service standards have declined. Local business units have been replaced by uniform call centres. These are character-istics of a world that has lived beyond its means.

Pay-up time reverses the 'something for nothing' culture. As the economy stagnates, so those businesses that have cut corners to sell at marginal cost disappear. In consumer shopping, the cheapest price may be bad news, since it raises the chance of a business collapse that will deny ongoing service. This is the broad background now unfolding as the greatest crash proceeds.

Businesses choose between volume at a low margin, or quality at a higher margin; between going for growth, ignoring quality, or building a business steadily, maintaining quality. These are normal choices for businesses to make. As a business, Britain went overboard for volume and growth in the period from the mid-1990s through to the bursting of the bubble in 2007. Bankers mortgaged the future by lending money unwisely, declaring profits without consideration of the losses that would inevitably follow, all in accordance with accounting standards. Few have the

4

financial resilience to cope with a financial crisis. Governments are in much the same state as many households and businesses. Bust.

A world riddled with contradictions

Policy contradictions also show us that the financial system has reached a roadblock. The glaring conflict between bailout and austerity is at the core. Each bailout or stimulus requires creation of more credit, leading to false financial speculation, and for a short while markets recover their poise. The threat of inflation returns. Later, bad debts rise, the markets tumble again and a new crisis emerges. Austerity, the alternative policy, cuts spending thereby cutting the immediate level of economic activity and bringing economic decline more quickly than the stimulus alternative. Whichever way they turn, the authorities are damned.

The world economy lurches from one crisis to another, driven by waves of artificial credit followed by distress as the costs of extra debt come to light. Governments are so frightened of the financial equivalent of detoxification – deflation – that they return every time to the rescue, never considering the longer term consequence. And as the debt burden grows so the crises come around more frequently, bringing greater destructive power with each success-ive cycle.

As the European debt crisis unfolded early in 2010, *The Economist* noted a contradiction. Impose austerity to balance the books and countries such as Greece would slide back into recession, yet stimulate any further and debt would become unaffordable[9].

The system limit explains why contradictions such as this keep appearing. The European debt crisis is but a minor part of the entire policy nettle. Ever since the credit interlude[10] started in the aftermath of the 1987 stock market crash, short-term panaceas have been adopted producing apparent prosperity, while the underlying contradictions have been waiting to be discovered. These underlying contradictions include the inability to balance public services, taxation, borrowing and regulation; and the desire to regulate banks more, thereby restricting their lending further, shrinking the global economy and making it even harder to repay debt.

Bankers have been set up as the fall guys to cover for what I see as a gross failure of political leadership. Nobody was able to see the whole picture thanks to delegated government and a forest of detail that obscured the simple point: it all depended on constant credit creation. A veritable troupe of other actors joined the easy money party:

- ◆ accountants adopted standards that restricted judgment, and regulators demanded conformity with those standards;

- ◆ economists and financial academics invented elaborate models that erroneously assumed financial markets follow the normal distribution;

- ◆ governments imposed increased overheads on the productive economy and measured the rise in overheads as economic growth;

- ◆ the public borrowed way beyond any prudent level in

the belief that debt could expand indefinitely at no cost;

◆ banks pushed credit out and gambled that it would be repaid.

Speculation was encouraged even when there was no economic purpose. Consider the relationships between investment banks, private equity, derivatives, hedge funds, commodity trading and private finance. What did they all have in common? Speculation – fed by debt based financial engineering. There was little economic substance to many of these investments.

The policy limit

When the world has previously hit a financial limit, new policies have emerged. The gold standard limited trade and deflated economies in the Great Depression; it was abandoned in the post-1945 Bretton Woods formula which adopted fixed exchange rates but limited the freedom of movement of capital. That, in turn, gave way to an era of floating exchange rates, which freed up capital movement.

There is an interaction between exchange rate policy, monetary policy and capital controls. If a country wants to have fixed exchange rates, then it cannot run an independent monetary policy as well as allowing free movement of capital: one of these has to be sacrificed to maintain the exchange rate. Likewise, a country that wants to run an independent monetary policy must choose between fixed exchange rates and free movement of capital, because an independent monetary policy together with free movement of capital will result in fluctuating exchange rates.

For the same reason, a country that wants free movement of capital cannot have fixed exchange rates and an independent monetary policy.

Fixed exchange rates, free movement of capital and independent monetary policies are in a three-way contradiction: only two can be satisfied at any time. This contradiction has long been known and understood but the contradictions causing and resulting from the financial system limit and the roadblock are not yet understood. However, they are significant.

I need also to scotch some myths.

Lending more to those who cannot pay, in order to buy time, is foolish. If a country cannot afford its debts, how will adding to those debts with more loans make a country more able to pay its way? If a household cannot afford its existing debt, why should it borrow more?

Reverting to capital controls would be effective in stopping deliberate monetary expansion. However, without continued credit expansion, the austerity contradiction would take effect: repaying debt drives economies downhill.

Returning to a gold standard would shrink the supply of credit, thereby severely deflating economies, bringing widespread misery. Going back to the past this way is not possible.

Recycling past policies will be equally ineffective in removing the system limit. It is time for fundamental change.

It is fashionable for economists and politicians to talk about rebalancing the global economy, as if some magical improvement can be obtained. I believe that trade and financial imbalances merely reflect the great credit bubble we have lived through. How can imbalances be removed other than by selective application of more credit or selective application of austerity? The system limit prevents rebalancing.

The entire post-1945 era of managed economies, culminating in the twenty-year credit interlude, and the absurd consumerist concept that the good times would roll for ever, is over. Nothing can bring it back.

The choice is between allowing the greatest crash ever to continue to build in force, or taking a unified grip on our institutional arrangements, our financial obligations and our way of life, in an attempt to find a completely original solution. These are the issues that *The Greatest Crash* explores.

2 Evolution by trial and error

How the financial system evolved

The banking system was invented in Florence, Genoa, Naples and Venice, those nation States that became Italy half a millennium later. The early bankers took in deposits and lent them out to finance trade, creating bills of exchange to be presented in correspondent banks in other nation States. Trade prospered as the means to finance and pay for it became established across national and geographic boundaries.

Originally, money consisted of gold and silver coins[11]. Their worth, both as a medium of exchange and as a store of value, was accepted widely. Prices fluctuated for natural causes, but there was no such thing as economic management. Accounts were kept in simple ledgers, debit and credit, assets and liabilities, income and expenditure, profit and loss. The financial system grew through a process akin to natural selection; it was never designed[12].

Starting with tulip mania in Holland, the financial system was prey to boom and bust. People have always used money to chase rainbows and every financial crash has been driven by a short-term cycle of greed followed by fear. The boom part of the cycle occurs when expanding credit allows fashionable buying, with the fashion itself driving prices up and attracting more buyers. The bust part of the cycle follows when selling takes over, prices fall and debts have to be honoured[13].

Evolution did have the benefit of fixing errors along the way. The original precious metal currency, which used silver and gold coins, proved to be a limit, so it was replaced by paper currency. This change was associated with the second major dislocation in the system, namely the South Sea bubble and John Law's Mississippi scheme.

On 12th July 1720, the Privy Council dismissed 18 petitions relating to bubble companies and abolished 86 existing companies by declaring them illegal. Britain's South Sea bubble drew to a close, leaving the credit system wrecked for most of the eighteenth century. In the preface to his original (1841) edition of *Extraordinary Popular Delusions and the Madness of Crowds*, Charles Mackay wrote "The object ... has been ... to show how easily the masses have been led astray." In his second (1852) edition, Mackay wrote "Sober nations have all at once become desperate gamblers, and risked almost their existence upon the turn of a piece of paper."[14]

Governments attempted to manage the financial system to reduce the tendency to boom and bust. The creation of central banks was part of the process of replacing raw market forces by political control. The Federal Reserve only dates from 1913, while the Bank of England was a private sector body until nationalised in 1946, although it was effectively a central bank long before.

During the financial crash of the 1930s, Britain chose to finally abandon the link with gold[15]. Instead, Britain adopted a system of book entry by which governments retained the power to control the rate of monetary expansion through a variety of tools limiting bank lending. Among those tools for managing the economy, was the 'corset' which forced banks to deposit funds with the Bank of England. Another allowed banks to absorb risk by making secret transfers to hidden reserves prior to publishing their accounts. Only in the post-1945 era were the tools gradually abandoned, allowing the quantity of credit in circulation to rise. Minimum liquidity ratios of 8% cash and 30% of all liquid assets were gradually abandoned, leading slowly to an inability to absorb serious losses.

However, America retained the fixed exchange rate with gold for another forty years after the Great Depression[16]. It was the loss of the relationship between the dollar and gold in 1971 that enabled the Federal Reserve to provide the means for American governments to manipulate the economy through credit creation, delivering apparently boundless prosperity. The earlier desire to moderate raw market forces was replaced by economic management through monetary and fiscal policies.

The system we have today simply evolved from the activities of those early bankers. As finance progressed, the concept of fractional credit appeared. Banks lent more than their deposit base, confident that not everyone would ask for their money back at the same time. But when crises threatened, exactly this happened, with the dreaded run on the bank. Bank failures were part of the evolutionary nature of the system.

The Marxist view of capitalism

The Marxists understood the system limit: their credo was that capitalism would self-destruct. Marx thought that capitalism would develop economic forces beyond its power to contain, and encouragement of growth would lead to more social opposition. Marxism foresaw a long chain of events, in which the internal contradictions of capitalism would lead to its downfall. Increased competition would drive workers' wages down to subsistence levels. Profits would fall and large companies would swallow up small companies. More people would be forced into the working class, causing the capitalist system to lead to greater divisions in society. There would be more and more severe economic crises. Reduced to a degraded condition, workers would then rise up in revolution and overthrow the system.

Some of these points seem relevant to today's economic and social conditions. But the Marxists also thought there would be a falling rate of profit caused by depletion of investment opportunities. They did not consider the possibility that radical change could occur as a result of innovation, provided that finance could be found. Nonetheless, the present state of finance fits the Marxist definition of forces that cannot be contained and therefore stifles innovation while it lasts. There are indeed greater divisions between haves and have-nots in the world today. The Marxists' error may have been that their timing was out by a matter of a century, over half of which can be ascribed to governments managing economies by expanding credit.

The Great Depression and Keynes
The Victorian era brought growth and scientific advance, but nonetheless the boom and bust cycle continued through the 19th century and into the early part of the 20th century. What we now

call the 'Great Depression' marked a turning point.

The Great Depression began as part of the usual boom and bust cycle, driven by fashionable buying of shares and property and the ready availability of credit to finance those purchases. Governments responded to events by cutting back spending, which set off a spiral of decline. Keynes showed the way out, managing demand by what we now call injecting money, so that the declines were halted and recovery started. As a result, it is now widely believed that it is mistaken to cut spending in a recession and governments can manage their way out of any decline by reflating, creating more credit. This is the basis of Quantitative Easing.

However, Keynes advocated cutting back the stimulus when times were good. He recognised that pump priming in recessions needed the opposite action in the good times – his formula for continued prosperity required governments to do as much to damp down any boom as to stimulate demand in a recession. Governments, however, were reluctant to constrain economies and face the voters' wrath; instead, economic management began to be seen as *always* neutering the forces of recession by providing more liquidity. But in the 1930s the world was not up against the system limit in the way it is now and therefore credit expansion worked its wonder.

The long economic cycle

Anyone who has been in business will be aware of the nature of the short-term economic cycle. During the expansionary part of the cycle credit increases and, of course, everyone feels good. The cycle then turns; recession follows. The short-term economic cycle is traditionally associated with the accumulation and disposal of physical goods – manufactured products and stock held by retailers[17].

It seems that there is also a much longer cycle, beyond the practical experience of our working lifetimes – a long wave that encompasses a cycle of fifty to eighty years, long periods of expansion followed by periods of contraction.

Various pioneers explored the concept that there is such a cycle in economies. One of the earliest was a Dr. Hyde Clarke, who published research on the food production cycle in 1847. A Russian Marxist, Pravus, published a correlation of price and business cycles in 1901[18]. There was further work by Van Gelderen and De Wolff in Holland. The real master, though, was Kondratieff, whose work appeared in the 1920s.

Kondratieff established that the long cycle is of variable periodicity (you may see references to 54 years, but this was Dr. Hyde Clarke's theory). In the growth phase, most years are prosperous; whereas in the contracting phase, few years are prosperous. Kondratieff also argued that agriculture suffers a pronounced depression in the contracting period. New inventions and developments proliferate, but cannot be exploited until the next growth phase.

Since the 1720s, that is, since the time of the South Sea bubble and Mississippi scheme, it is possible to trace five long cycles. The first cycle, from 1720 to about 1780, involved recovery from the damage done by those manias, followed by the Industrial

Revolution and a depression. In the second cycle, from 1780 to 1840, canals were built and the textile trade expanded. This was followed by a price collapse.

The third cycle (1840 to 1896) started with the railway era, which led the way into the great Victorian expansion. The cycle finished with a decline marked by the first Barings crisis. From 1896 to 1940 came the rise of the motor car, South American defaults, the Roaring Twenties and again a depression. The South American defaults of 1920/21 marked a turning point, with the Roaring Twenties being a period of easy credit and false prosperity, much as we saw in the years prior to the credit crunch. Despite (or perhaps as a result of) the creation of the Federal Reserve, the Great Depression was somewhat worse than all prior depressions since the financial crash of the 1720s.

After 1945, in the fifth cycle, governments set out to prove that they could manage economies to deliver constantly rising living standards and full employment. Their economic policy levers all caused expansion of the credit supply.

Each long cycle can be broken down into four components, i.e.

(1) a period of expansion, usually accompanied by rising prices; then

(2) a warning shot, some sort of temporary financial dislocation, that gives way to

(3) renewed good times, but

(4) the renewed good times do not last, ending in a depression, with falling prices and contraction of the credit supply.

The western financial system now seems to me to be more unstable than America's was prior to the Great Depression. In America, at the start of the 1930s, there was about $30 book entry in the banking system for every $1 of cash. The wave of bank failures reduced credits, while write-offs reduced debts, so that by 1934 this ratio was down to 10:1. Today, the debt to currency ratio can no longer be measured accurately, because there is so much offshore and shadow banking that escapes measurement. The part that can be measured suggests the debt to currency ratio may now be more like 100:1.

Now I would like to turn to property, which has its own boom and bust cycle. Here are some figures[18] about residential development land prices:

1892 – 95	£130 per acre
1920	£900
1922	£250
1969	£10,000

It is fascinating to note how often property is involved in financial dislocations. Property is illiquid: you can only sell it well in the good times, when people are clamouring to buy. And it serves as collateral for debt.

A plot of development land in Florida sold for $1,500 in 1914. Twelve years later, similar plots fetched $1.5 million. After the crash that followed, it took 35 years to recoup the losses.

In the last quarter century, it has been fashionable to debunk Kondratieff, the usual argument being that there has been no visible peak of activity followed by a severe downturn. This is exactly the same error made by those who believe that share prices always rise because they have risen for so many years in the past: it fails to allow for the credit interlude that started twenty-four years ago and is now drawing to a close. This is an understandable error, but in my view the cyclical extension brought about as a result of the credit interlude created by the Federal Reserve in 1987 and continued to this day, has only made the ensuing depression later, longer and deeper than it might have been.

The lesson of long cycles from the past is simple, if a little unwelcome. Over some four centuries, periods of inflation have been followed by periods of deflation. Since the end of World War Two, the world has experienced the greatest inflation ever. Yet the post-1945 inflation is an aberration in both amplitude and duration. The greatest inflation of all and the longest peace time prosperity were bought with the tool of easy credit. The end of easy credit spells an end to the methods and results of the past sixty years and hence to this extended Kondratieff cycle. The unwelcome lesson from history is that the greatest deflation should follow.

The post-war consensus and the managed economy

Any thought that a long economic cycle might exist was dismissed throughout the post-war era. Because governments set out to manage economies and avoid the perceived mistakes of the Great Depression, it was widely believed that a new economic era had arrived. The political consensus became: the tools of economic management will allow governments to deliver continuous growth. For about half a century, the golden nirvana did seem to have arrived.

As governments managed exchange rates and interest rates to blunt any recession and acquire ballot-box popularity, the economic cycles of past centuries were quickly forgotten. Nobody realised the significance of relentless expansion of the monetary aggregates. Keynes' advice to damp down any boom was ignored. Along with the continued expansion, inflation rose as the increased availability of credit pulled the global economy along faster than natural growth. This also was cyclical, since the rate of inflation came tumbling down in the 1979-to-1982 recession, turned up towards 10% in 1990, then crashed down to new lows. One of the obvious lessons of recent events is that the managed economy, driven by credit expansion, no longer works as well as it did.

The growth of services and a new cycle

Britain's manufacturing base has shrunk and the British economy today is dominated by services, notably financial services and consumption, the latter itself being mainly retail spending. Britain's last deep recession was in 1990 - 1992. To encapsulate the economic cycle entirely, it should run either from the trough of the 1990-1992 recession to the trough of the 2007-2009 crisis, or alternatively, it could be measured from the peak in summer 1989 through to the peak in early 2007. The point is that a complete economic cycle includes a recession and a speculative boom. It appears to me that in 2005, the Treasury assumed that only half the cycle (the half without a recession) was really a complete economic cycle[19].

In agricultural economies, the economic cycle was driven by the seasons and the weather; weather goes in a multi-year cycle. When the Industrial Revolution displaced agriculture, manufacturers started to build stocks (inventory, in the American terminology). Stocks were not always sold quickly and so a stock building cycle came to drive the short-term economy. Manufacturers who built up stocks were surprised when demand slipped; they then cut prices to sell their surplus. The agricultural cycle of weather and seasons gave way to the manufacturing cycle of accumulation and reduction of physical stock.

Today's economy is built on services. Service industries have no physical inventory. Instead, capacity expands and contracts with the economic cycle. A service business has to provide capacity at the point at which it is needed. During the expansionary part of the cycle, service businesses add new capacity. When recession comes along, that surplus capacity acts as a drag on business and has to be cut back.

As an example, consider the shiny new computers and websites that the on-line stock broking industry acquired in 1998 and 1999. By 2001, following the dot-com disaster and the 'go nowhere' nature of the main equity markets, the number of bargains (market trades) had fallen to roughly half what it was at the peak.

The volume of business to pay for all those new gadgets was simply not around.

I believe that the stock market losses of 2000-2003 were just a taster. Markets have been erratic, responding first to financial stimulus then to the resulting debt problems. This great bear market may run and run. As investors slowly learn what life is like in a bear market, one in which the overall trend of prices is downwards with steep falls followed by long rallies, sometimes lasting years, with more good days than bad, so securities trading activity will fall and stay down.

The diagram *(fig. 1)* shows the conceptual nature of the cycle (it does not refer specifically to any industry). Rising demand draws more players into the game. In the early stages, services are delivered personally: they have to be available at the point of demand. Gradually, individual services are replaced by mass service providers who acquire fixed costs (computers, premises, people – they are no longer a variable cost) and when the recession comes round, only price competition to get volume is possible. Not everyone can earn enough contribution to those fixed costs from a price war. The result is inevitable.

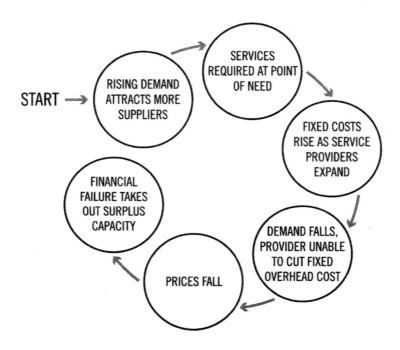

Fig. 1 The service industry capacity cycle

The expansion and contraction of service businesses now forms a significant short-term economic cycle, unrecognised in many text books[20].

3   Before the credit crunch

Borrowing from the future

Britain last emerged from an age of austerity in the early 1950s, stimulated by rebuilding the economy and exports[21]. Rationing was swept away and a long period of expansion began. A number of major changes happened: first manufacturing prospered, led by the motor car industry, then living standards and consumer spending rose. The rise in consumer spending went hand in hand with a general feeling of prosperity which led to higher imports, the subsequent decline of British manufacturing and the rise of the consumerist lobby. Governments deliberately reflated their way out of any recession and increased flows of credit appeared, sometimes in the run up to any significant election.

Over a period of half a century, Britain gradually transformed itself into a regulated consumer society. Consumption became the dominant economic activity. Since credit was the driving force, debt levels rose and inflation arrived. Banking standards were gradually relaxed and bank capital levels allowed to fall, with the result that lending continued to expand and the feel-good factor spread. Governments, ever happy to claim the benefit, sat back and allowed the great credit boom to gather force.

From 1982 the credit boom picked up speed and ran, with minor interruptions, until it reached its natural end a quarter of a century later with the credit crunch. The proceeds of higher lending were circulating and generating extra tax revenue, so silly stories abounded circa 1988 and again circa 1999 that the British government would repay all its debt. Nobody noticed that the government was prospering financially because private sector debt was rising fast. The surpluses that government achieved were not banked; instead, they were spent creating more overheads as the regulated society developed. From the government's point of view, much of the regulatory growth was 'off balance sheet' as it was farmed out to a variety of agencies. Some of the growth in regulatory overhead was incurred by the private sector, leading to growth in what were essentially unproductive overheads being erroneously classified as economic growth.

Another side effect was that asset markets boomed, creating false expectations of easy money. Pension funds declared financial surpluses based on the overvalued levels of stock markets; businesses and governments cut pension contributions[22]; and over-generous early retirement terms were offered to some. Thus were the seeds of the present pensions crisis sown.

Resources were probably misused in the boom, and the worries now appearing about the environment are one consequence. Environmentalists believe resources have been wasted and the planet destroyed. Another theory is that economic growth has been driven by easily achievable steps that cannot be repeated, such as industrialisation and better education[23]. Social benefits were allowed to grow. Long-term commitments were taken on, based on the expansionary environment. Across the board, Britain literally mortgaged its future. Both public and private debt grew too much.

The consumer society of the last half century was founded on borrowing from the future. Policies that amount to creating more credit and encouraging more debt, bring short-term relief at the price of strengthening and lengthening the downward side of the cycle, as the additional debt falling due adds to the interest burden to be serviced and repaid. This is why injecting more purchasing power via monetary expansion causes its own failure once the initial benefit wears off.

How the British economy destroyed value

In 2004, I attended an economic presentation. I expected this to be a conventional analysis and, to some extent, my expectation was realised. Reams of graphs were shown demonstrating that there was an incipient slowdown in the global economy, with different causes in different regions. The speaker drew the comfortable conclusion that the rate of economic growth in the UK would ease off but still be about 2% to 3%. He went on to forecast falling corporate profits with a further rise in the stock market as interest rates peaked and turned down again. Notice the lack of logic in this: falling corporate profits ought to be reflected in *lower* share prices.

Among that speaker's charts was one showing the growth of what I call broad money (that is, all types of lending), running at just over 12% per annum. I believe that the majority of this credit growth has been unproductive. To see why, we need to understand the concept of the economic multiplier.

The economic multiplier is the amount of economic activity generated by one currency unit of investment. In an expanding economy, £1 of extra lending when invested should generate more than £1 of economic activity. In Britain, in the years before the bubble burst, £1 extra lending produced about 25p inflation and 10p economic growth[24]. Expanding the money supply was counter-productive, rather than an aid to total growth. The unmeasured two-thirds of monetary growth was probably wasted in servicing existing debts, adding to them or boosting asset prices.

Since debt was growing at roughly ten times the rate of economic growth, it follows that in aggregate, the British financial system was already destroying value before the headlines of August 2007. This financial destruction was masked while Britons were still able to borrow furiously and spend their borrowed money, because spending borrowed money was measured as economic growth.

The economy is measured by Gross Domestic Product (GDP) which is estimated from surveys of pay, construction activity, motor trade stocks, retail stocks and so on. It is an attempt to measure all national income from activities within the country. In a healthy economy, GDP growth plus inflation should be more than growth in the money supply. In Britain, the sum of the GDP rise plus inflation has been around one third of monetary growth for many years. Far from being prosperous, Britain is financially unstable when the entire picture is considered. Keynesian reflation cannot work if debt continually grows faster than the economy. For the same reason, creating more credit via Special Drawing Rights cannot work.

The story was similar in America for the same reasons. GDP was expanding at 5% or 6% per annum including inflation, but lending grew at over 10% per annum. The surge in borrowing accounted for the rise in both stock markets and property markets. Either the permanent loss of output following recession will now cause the borrowing orgy to unravel, or unravelling property and stock markets will strengthen the recessionary forces: a chicken and egg problem – it does not matter which occurs first.

One bank's lending is another person's borrowing and when spent, becomes a third person's income. All that borrowed money has been spent. The growth in borrowing was the main cause of economic activity, as well as the cause of inflation. It now seems that some of those who borrowed could not afford their debt service cost in any but the most prosperous economic climate and hence arrears and repossessions are slowly mounting[25]. Perhaps they also did not understand what the obligations of debt entailed. Here is one of many contradictions: do we blame those who borrowed for creating a debt problem or thank them for creating the prosperity we have now lost?

What happens when borrowing stops expanding? There will be less money flowing round the economy for others to regard as their income. So a recession must automatically follow. Perversely, if people save rather than spend, or borrow less than they were doing, then this is also very bad economic news. We shall examine this further in chapter 5. Good news is also bad news when governments encourage more mal-investment with credit expansion.

The US had a similar credit boom to Britain, but there was one difference. In the US, financial sector debt formed a slightly bigger proportion of the total because it was growing in line with other debt, whereas in the UK, the debt growth was concentrated more on consumers and mortgages. Put another way, American banks binged first on the Enrons and Parmalats of this world, then more recently on proprietary trading, while British banks feasted on their traditional diets of home owners and commercial property.

The credit system has now turned the monetary tap off and governments are desperately trying to turn it on again with tools such as Quantitative Easing. Clearly people can no longer borrow and spend so freely, which has brought a lower level of economic activity to the world. As we now know, the tap was turned off by the rise in the price of home loans, leading to defaults, uncertainty about which bank was hiding what losses, and the consequent shrinkage of wholesale inter-bank lending. Endless financial crises, for which Greece, Ireland, Portugal and the Euro are tasters, will now follow.

The Private Finance Initiative

The idea behind the Private Finance Initiative (PFI) was to replace public capital expenditure plus ongoing operating costs by the purchase of a complete service package. Any private capital introduced in this way would not count as public sector borrowing.

PFI started with roads, which have high construction costs compared to ongoing maintenance, and prisons, where there was a political objective to introduce private security guards in prisons detaining lower risk offenders. After the 1997 general election, the concept spread into hospital and school construction. However, clinical care and teaching were to remain the province of the State, with just building maintenance and support services, such as catering, bought in as a service package.

The service fee payable to each PFI contractor includes an element of interest on capital. The historical rate of interest has fluctuated around 2% to 3% in real terms for centuries. According to the Office of Health Economics (an independent research body), PFI projects were compared with conventional Exchequer finance using a discount rate of 6%. However, the Office of Health Economics believed the discount rate should be 4%, while the Institute for Public Policy Research preferred 5%. The discount rate allows for the time value of money: £100 received one year in the future discounted at 4% is equivalent to having £96.15 today. A higher discount rate makes annual servicing costs appear more attractive than upfront capital costs.

Given that levels of interest rates have fluctuated frequently, there is little reason to suppose that a forward thirty-year forecast can be accurate. My concern is that the world is moving, slowly but surely, into a deflationary future and therefore the service fees payable in PFI projects will gradually become excessive. The long-term effect of deflation will be that eventually servicing costs will prove more expensive in real terms. To this extent, such long-term contracts are likely to prove poor value for the public purse, albeit highly profitable for their financiers.

The problem of long-term large scale project costing is well known in the defence industry. The established method of paying for defence supply contracts is to apply a cost recovery formula after the event. If the contractor was then deemed to have made excess profit, the excess profit could and would be clawed back. Such provisions are strikingly absent from the Private Finance Initiative.

Other warnings

These were not the only shortcomings of PFI. In schools, Local Education Authorities bought contracts to design, build and operate new schools, which were imposed on school governors on the principle 'there is no alternative' and also without consideration for long-term fluctuation in demand caused by demographic change affecting school populations.

In hospitals, the King's Fund[26] argued that new hospitals were being built without regard to how they would fit into the overall health service framework. Primary and community services were not part of the usual hospital PFI project of building works. New hospital capital projects worth £1.4 billion were agreed before the National Bed Inquiry reported. The government said that the number of beds needed to increase, yet every PFI hospital project involved a planned reduction in beds[27].

PFI was a financial bubble

Financial bubbles involve easy money spent unwisely, grand projects of uncertain value and creative accounting to avoid putting the true financing cost onto a balance sheet as a liability. All of these appeared to be present in PFI. The problems that have arisen with PFI as the years go by, together with the further difficulty of raising finance in the credit crunch, only reinforce this view. The total present value of all PFI liabilities is not clear: only building capital values have been admitted by the Treasury[28].

Private equity

PFI was effective at allowing costs of finance to be hidden off balance sheet. Private equity used a different accounting method. It involved extensive borrowing, used to finance equity purchases, with some of the debt borrowed by the takeover target rather than the buying company. I was brought up to believe that to buy something you needed the cash, but the chain of loans involved in private equity has enabled the buyer to use the takeover target to provide some of its finance. By elaborate alchemy, private equity managed to twist debt around so that the target company in a takeover partly funded the bidder. In a non-bubble economy, of course, all costs of takeover finance would be borne by the acquiring company. What this shows is the folly of dividing complex financial arrangements into small parcels, losing sight of the big picture.

Debt created when private equity firms took over companies was marketed to pension funds, retail banks, insurance companies and the like and thus appeared in the portfolios of funds investing in corporate bonds. All of these investors wished to earn a high rate of interest. The investors in debt and the owners of the purchased businesses had opposing objectives. Investors hungry for interest wanted their cake to last for ever while owners wanted a fast capital gain and exit. There was a fundamental conflict of interest between the owners and capital providers. During the boom years of private equity much heat and light was spun about making businesses more efficient, without ever explaining how a business that has extra debt to service can be more efficient.

The flip side of private equity is that corporate bonds have become far, far riskier – and it is rather hard to analyse the risks[29]. This is similar to *kaizen*, the financial engineering that gripped Japanese businesses in the 1980s before the Tokyo stock market entered its long decline. Private equity has been described as a clumsy trick[30]. More than one quarter of companies owned by private equity and sold off in 2007 have gone bankrupt[31].

4   An era of wishful thinking

The last twenty years or so have been characterised by extensive wishful thinking. Here are some examples of policy errors, by no means a full list:

◆   Policy makers believed that financial bubbles could not be recognised at the time, so they should be allowed to happen then the mess cleared up afterwards.

◆   Policy makers believed that debt could expand indefinitely, at no cost.

◆   The lessons of Japan's lost decade (now already two decades) were ignored.

◆   Nobody realised that interest rate rises would make existing borrowing unaffordable and cause a wave of defaults.

◆   Politicians suffered from the delusion that they could pull mysterious policy levers to achieve any political and economic objective.

◆   Accountants believed that by following precise standards businesses could be compared like for like, removing judgment. Regulators then demanded obedience to accounting standards, with the result that financial prudence (the ability for accounts to recognise reality) was abolished[32].

◆   The world was swamped with so many detailed requirements and standards that nobody could understand how they all fitted together. It was assumed that 'transparency', i.e. extensive detail, would solve the inability to comprehend how the parts made the whole.

♦   Politicians counted the immediate results of the debt spree as growth, ignoring the future cost of servicing and repaying debt.

♦   Pension funds made unrealistically optimistic assumptions, such as that equities would achieve 8% growth per annum indefinitely.

♦   Financial theorists promoted formulae for how capital markets ought to work based on the mistaken assumption that price movements followed the normal distribution.

I will consider various aspects of this wishful thinking in this and the next two chapters. This chapter discusses some obvious lessons that are largely ignored, and examines failures in numeracy. Chapter 5 then examines various paradoxes and contradictions, and chapter 6 investigates the collective amnesia that is popularly called 'group think'.

Lessons from Japan

Japan's stagnation in the 1990s ought to have taught the world a lesson about policy options. In Japan, every policy option recommended by experts failed after a couple of years. After the Japanese bubble burst in 1990, the authorities tried to fix the Japanese financial system using looser monetary policy. Monetary policy achieved little. Interest rates tumbled yet a minor economic recovery soon petered out. Fiscal policy and political reform also failed. **There are no easy policy options** because none tackle the real underlying problem of too much debt. There is still too much debt in Japan, as there is in the rest of the world economy today.

It is worth noting that accounting for bad debts is done somewhat differently in Japan. There, it is customary for banks to support businesses that are unable to service their debts by waiving interest charges. It has been fashionable to criticise the Japanese system of banks giving life support to businesses, yet it seems to me that there is another lesson here: financial contracts may not always align with the broad interest of society.

Warnings from sub-prime

When US house prices started falling in autumn 2006, the usual commentaries appeared, proclaiming a soft landing. New Century's Chapter 11 bankruptcy filing was soon followed by opinions saying that sub-prime would not affect the broader economy. Then the world learned that the problem was much deeper. It appeared that the value of 'teaser' or special terms mortgages outside the sub-prime sector had, in recent years, been similar to the value of sub-prime lending. I believe that some 20% of lending on US housing had been sub-prime and a further 20% involved some form of special introductory offer. Much of the remainder was what Britons call second mortgages ('piggyback' in the American jargon) and therefore also high risk.

It took under a year from the early signs of distress, which I noted when visiting the United States in May 2006, to New Century filing for bankruptcy. Sub-prime gave the world seven general warnings:

◆ bad debts spread slowly but surely;

◆ vested interests can fail to foresee the broader effect;

◆ fringe lenders may hit financial difficulty;

◆ property investors find they face default – and generally do not realise the risk;

◆ there is no reason to believe the course of events will be greatly different in the UK compared to the US;

◆ if it looks like a pack of cards and feels like a pack of cards, then it *is* a pack of cards;

◆ what lies below the surface of any investment package may be anything but obvious.

Most people who borrow money on a mortgage for property subscribe to the belief that house prices always go up and therefore they can gear up their investment with debt. Rising defaults give the lie to this.

Until about ten years ago, if you borrowed from a bank or building society, you assumed that your loan was from that lender and you paid them back. Relationships between borrower and lender changed in the final years of the credit boom. Lenders 'securitised' their loan books and sold the derived fixed interest security on to others via the investment banking fraternity, and therefore lost contact with their borrowers' ability to afford debt. Securities were offered at various risk levels, under a number of fancy titles. Nobody knew quite what the risk levels really were, nor just how strong the security would prove in a downturn, which is how the investment banking industry caused damage to the broad economy. Securitisation converted the loans buying property into low-grade fixed interest stocks, which no doubt appeared in corporate bond funds and such like. Securitised loans were also bought by hedge funds anxious to boost their yields.

As well as securitising lending, investment banks manage hedge funds. So one department of an investment bank may have been providing the capital to sub-prime lenders, while another was buying the securitised loans on the other side of the balance sheet. Meanwhile, a third department may have been doing the securitisation deals. Of course, it may be that these departments were in different banks but the principle is the same. The numbers are pretty opaque and hard to interpret, because so many banks were lending to each other as well as lending directly to buyers of sub-prime property.

The misuse of numbers and bubble accounting

Throughout the credit interlude, ever stranger ways were found of expressing economic concepts in numbers. These were not deliberate breaches of accounting standards. The direction in which standards evolved enabled the economic substance of businesses to be subdivided into meaningless elements, some of which can only be described as 'bubble accounting'. I have collected some examples of these strange ways of measurement. They span accounting, economic and public policy matters.

Wherever you look, there are examples of the misuse of numbers. Some of my examples demonstrate limits to statistics or to the interpretation often given to statistics. Other examples identify specific areas where standards may have limitations. One of the problems of the 21st century is the vast explosion of detail, which serves only to obscure basic principles.

My starting point is the principle used in accounting for the treatment of machinery compared to accounting for the skill and knowledge of people.

<u>Accounting for knowledge</u>

Knowledge and skill are now essential parts of any organisation's value. Yet the way accountants measure capital is based on the factory worker tending expensive machinery. Take, for example, a chair. It's pretty obvious that a chair is to sit on. It is also a capital asset that counts in the balance sheet and should be depreciated at, say, 25% per annum. So the money paid for a new chair is part of the 'value' created by any business.

But what about the person who sits on that chair? Aren't people worth some value in a business that depends on intellectual skill? No, according to accounting standards, the person is worthless. The business has legal ownership of the chair but not of a person.

Accountancy is still stuck in the era when workers sweated at textile looms. The loom was relatively expensive, difficult to build and had to be scrapped when worn out. There was an endless supply of labourers seeking work as the Industrial Revolution progressed. If one fell sick, the mill owner hired another person, by the hour if necessary. The twin concepts of fixed assets needing depreciation (high expenditure up front, spread over some years) and labour as a disposable cost suited the Industrial Revolution.

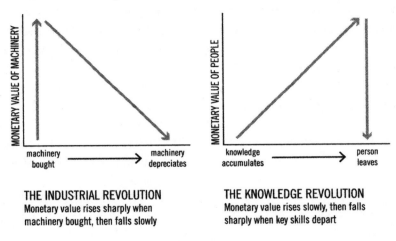

THE INDUSTRIAL REVOLUTION
Monetary value rises sharply when
machinery bought, then falls slowly

THE KNOWLEDGE REVOLUTION
Monetary value rises slowly, then falls
sharply when key skills depart

Fig. 2 How capital formation has changed

But now we have the Knowledge Revolution. Work is about the ability to accumulate and apply intellectual skill. The desk, the chair, the computer are now the incidentals: the person matters far more than the artefact. *Fig.* 2 contrasts capital formation in the Industrial Revolution and the Knowledge Revolution.

Accountants don't like measuring knowledge. There are few standards; the concept is subjective. The market has a way of correcting for such accounting limitations by valuing quoted knowledge businesses – consultancies, media enterprises and such like – above their book value.

Machinery is capitalised then written off over its useful life whereas people are treated as a direct or variable cost. However, people skills behave in exactly the opposite way to machinery: they are built gradually over a long period of time and lost in one fell swoop on resignation, retirement or death. So accounting for knowledge needs to be turned inside out by accumulating its value over the years and writing it off in one lump sum on resignation, retirement or death. The roles of machines and people have completely reversed and the flow of value into and out of economic capital has also reversed.

Accountants are not going to like changing their existing methods, nor will the taxation system[33]. But who would seriously believe that a chair has value and a human being does not?

What is a valuation?

If an asset is priced by competitive market activity, as happens for actively traded shares and bonds, then a fair price is known at any point in time[34]. The price may change, but a balance sheet showing assets and liabilities will be reliable at the date it is prepared. But when an asset is little traded, how is its price to be determined? Throughout the derivatives' world, prices are set only rarely in the market; most derivatives have to be valued artificially, often by a computer model. Given the scale of losses revealed in the banking system in 2007 and 2008, one has to observe that these models may not always be right[35]. Subjective valuations are more likely to produce losses when exposed to real markets. A technical paper that crossed my desk in late 2007 noted (as an example) that one particular financial instrument was valued in two completely different and contradictory ways by two different banks. Nobody said: "What's going on here?"

Luckily accounting standards impose 'mark to market' valuations in most cases where there is a market price. 'Mark to market' means that actual prices set in a competitive market are used. This stops the argument that there is some inherent worth that the market does not recognise. It does not eliminate the problem of computer-based guessing games, but it does mean that *some* financial assets have reliable valuations at a point in time. The securities industry does not like constraints on the guessing game and as a result there have been a number of demands to abandon market price valuations.

At the heart of the US Treasury's post Lehman bailout plan, lay an assumption that the market price of credit derivatives was too low and eventually higher values would be achieved. Market price is all we have to go on. In the mad rush to invent schemes to save the banking system from itself, the authorities have started to modify the application of mark to market accounting. This seems to be replacing the limited market data that exists, by conjecture as to the true worth of credit derivatives. If the low value of credit derivatives is anywhere near the truth, then it follows that the assumption of eventual higher worth will not last and therefore such bailouts will fail sooner or later.

There is a reasonable point that mark to market valuations exaggerated the boom and may now be exaggerating the bust, since prices were undoubtedly high in the boom years. Artificially over pricing by ignoring depressed prices in the bust can only set the pricing error in stone. Prudent accounting would avoid exaggeration in the good years and mark down any dubious assets in bad years. It seems to me that prudent and cautious accounting is now being subverted to the political need to pretend that things may be better than they are by suppressing mark to market at this point in the cycle. The majority of a bank's assets are loans that are not subject to mark to market accounting and may be overstated when consideration is given to the likely rise in bad debts over the next few years. If this is the case, then mark to market valuations may simply be limiting the extent of the over-statement[36].

Markets represent the sum of everyone's opinion about the future. Markets do not make statements about the present. If a market price is down, then there has to be a reason: future business prospects may have changed in some way. In the case of valuation of financial assets, the market is anticipating future defaults that will cause losses. The only issue will be the accuracy of the market's anticipation of future losses when they materialise several years hence. This is why 'mark to market' is so important and why the howls of anguish should be ignored.

It is strange that investment banks have readily adopted mark to market valuations for their own debt. This arises when a bank raises capital by issuing a loan stock and takes some of this stock on to its trading book. The market price drops because the market thinks the bank may default. The bank writes down that part of its own debt held on its trading book, writes down the larger obligation to repay the entire stock of debt and produces an instant profit! A little thought will show that the profit is artificial because it can only arise if the going concern assumption that underlies all accounting is breached. Why did accountants ever allow this[37]?

Risk is not amortised

Risk is a poorly understood financial concept. Mathematically, it means the probability of a particular outcome occurring. This is different from uncertainty, which cannot be quantified. As has been shown[2], there are defects in both the probability assumptions used to price risk and the probability of extreme unusual events. But there is another problem.

Across a broad portfolio of investments, risk is bound to strike somewhere, some time. Derivatives are usually carried at a value that is set by a computer model, but in aggregate they involve a much higher total exposure – the notional principal of the contracts. Since derivatives are a form of insurance policy, their market value will usually be only a percentage of the total 'sum assured' – and that sum assured is the notional principal liability (or asset) which each derivative represents. *In extremis*, notional principal liability can turn into real loss. It is a contingent risk[38] [39]. Accounting standards simply show it as a footnote to accounts.

To understand the significance of this, let's compare the principles of insurance and the principles of derivatives. Imagine a general insurer which charges a premium for the risk of a maximum possible claim value *(fig. 3)*. Financially, the insurer builds up reserves against future claims from some of its premium income and is able to protect itself from the risk of a high incidence of high value claims through reinsurance.

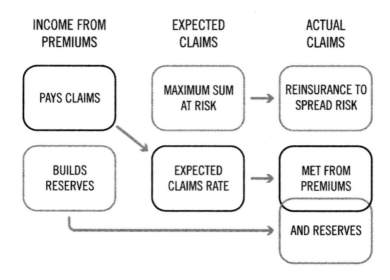

Fig. 3 How an insurance company spreads risk

Derivatives ought to be similar, but they are somewhat less prudent financially *(fig. 4)*. Unlike insurance, there is little published claims experience to go on, nor is any value put aside

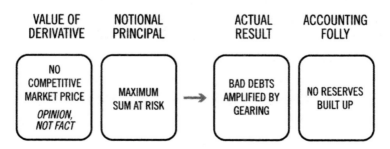

Fig. 4 How a derivative increases risk

annually for future losses. Having no financial reserves seems to me to be a financial folly that should be challenged. The valuation discrepancies reported, after the credit crunch emerged, indicated the risks and demonstrated that risk spreading was ineffective. The notional principal of derivatives is like the maximum claims value in insurance, while the market value is analogous to the premium paid. Yet notional principal is, in total, some nine times world Gross Domestic Product. How can the world have contingent financial liabilities to itself of as much as nine times world GDP[40]? Something is very wrong with derivatives.

Irrespective of the bad debt problem, the scale of derivatives needs to be reduced. Just like an insurer making financial provision for future claims, the owners of derivative liability positions ought to make financial provision for a bigger proportion of notional principal being lost in an extreme claim situation. Notional principal liabilities should be amortised by charging a proportion of the risk to profit each year, creating a bigger financial cushion against a catastrophic series of derivative losses. However, running down the risk in this way will take time and will itself make the economic contraction worse.

Offshore financial vehicles

The development of offshore, off-balance sheet financial vehicles played a part in the collapse of Enron. Accountants constructed elaborate standards which were rigorously followed yet produced nonsense. For example, Northern Rock had to feed Granite with new mortgage debt even though Granite appeared to be both independent and outside the jurisdiction for nationalisation.

The true effect of using offshore financial vehicles is to hide the real picture from enquiring minds, while enabling the growth of credit to continue unchecked and unrecognised. A more recent accounting proposal was to allow some, but not all, off balance sheet financial vehicles. It would be much better to put a complete stop to these financial hideaways.

The cost of debt

There is a long-standing problem with the British financial system. Income from dividends is treated as a distribution out of taxed profits and then partially taxed again when received by share-holders. The cost of interest on debt is tax deductible by a business. This biases businesses to use debt finance rather than equity finance. It is another contributing factor to the pickle that the British financial system is now in. The taxation system has had many 'reforms', mostly to find ways of taking more while *pretending* to take less. Putting equity and debt finance on an equal footing will hurt, but is necessary. Debt interest should not be tax deductible[41], and of equal importance, dividends should not be taxed twice.

Public or private debt?

In Britain and America, politicians claimed prudence (at least prior to the bailouts) in not borrowing extensively for the public purse, ignoring the huge debts that households and businesses had built up with their tacit encouragement. Private sector debt rose faster than economic growth. Government debt only rose modestly during the explosion in private sector debt and actually fell as a proportion of GDP. Private sector debt has already brought the British economy to its knees. Now the British

Government is trying to reduce public sector borrowing. The sum of *both* types of borrowing was too high and reducing either component will bring defaults.

The statistics of difference

Official sources choose how they present statistics to achieve a desired political effect. There is no factual error, but the casual observer is left to draw a conclusion which may be erroneous. Here is how it is done.

Suppose the economy goes into recession – as has happened – and manufacturing output declines by 9% year on year, while the whole economy (measured as a GDP estimate), declines by 4% over the same period. The 4% decline will get the headline treatment, while less mention will be made of the 9% decline. Now suppose that, in the next quarter, the level of manufacturing picks up by 1% so that the cumulative decline over the 15-month period is about 8.1%, while the whole economy picks up by 0.2%, so that the cumulative drop in total economic activity over the 15-month period is about 3.8%. Guess what? Headlines will scream "Recovery!" and "Economic growth returns!" Nobody mentions the permanent loss in output that has occurred. We will see a recent example of this in chapter 6.

This misleading effect is achieved by presenting statistics as year-on-year differences. Pundits comment quickly on the superficial picture, without having time to look beneath the surface. Short-term instability in capital markets, over time periods of hours, often results from superficial reactions to news items followed by a deeper look later.

The same behaviour can be observed with inflation statistics. Price levels are under severe pressure as the contractionary economic forces proceed, but drawing year on year comparisons gives equal weight to a change in prices a year earlier.

Bubble accounting must change

It is difficult for the layman to have any real understanding of the true financial risks affecting our society. Every little detail of financial accounting may be technically accurate yet the overall picture can be meaningless. To understand accounts, you need to get to grips with the myriad of accounting standards and then analyse their limitations. How many non-accountants understand the guessing game of valuations? Do the public understand that footnotes to some bank and corporate accounts may be disclosing real risks in derivatives? How is an investor to know the true ongoing worth of a business that depends on the skills of its people, when those skills are treated as worthless in the accounts? How can anyone have a true picture of a financial business if some of its liabilities are hidden in offshore financial vehicles?

Looking at the way economic statistics are interpreted, again there is both confusion and misleading comfort because the cost of debt used to buy economic growth is simply ignored. A monthly report of economic growth minus credit growth is needed. Over the past twenty years, such a measure would have shown severely negative returns. People might just take notice of the questionable state of our financial world if purported economic growth was shown in relation to the debt used to create it.

Politicians need to stop hoodwinking the public with empty

comparisons. It is time to end the misuse of numbers.

Pension funds

Pensions are topical. It is widely argued that consumers do not save enough for their pensions. Some may choose not to save, thanks to a lack of trust in the savings industry. Others cannot afford pension contributions because they are weighed down by borrowing costs, servicing their existing debts. We will investigate the broad relationship between debt, saving and economic prosperity in chapter 5.

Pension investment is a fashion business. Pension investment managers reacted to the great inflation of the 1960s and 1970s by stocking up with more equities. They continued to buy equities until the start of the dot-com bust. Now they are gradually cutting back, diverting some of their investments to commodities and fixed interest. Since pension funds form a major component of capital markets, the sheer weight of their buying (and selling) power will influence market trends.

Pension fund growth assumptions

Despite the move from defined benefit schemes, pension funds still represent the bedrock of savings and, therefore, fund valuations matter. If you belong to a defined benefit scheme, you have probably received various notices about actuarial valuations and funding percentages. The issues that matter are hidden in the small print.

Actuaries calculate the liabilities to pay pensions by estimating future returns and mortality rates. These days, a realistic and prudent rate of return for a fund with no equity investment would be about 3½%. So long as actual returns do not under-perform these returns for several years, valuations will be dominated by the estimates. The standard long-term assumptions made about equities have been shown to be incorrect[42], yet many pension funds continue to assume equity out-performance, giving the impression that any deficit is smaller and hence the funds will meet their liabilities. One ought (based on recent experience) to plan on the basis that equities are at least as likely to fall by 8% a year as rise by 8% a year, which has been a common assumption. Having such a realistic expectation, of course, would destroy pension funds completely.

Optimistic projections for future returns on pension investments are dangerous. There is an American example, described in an editorial in the *Wall Street Journal*: the Pension Benefit Guaranty Corporation, which is the US long stop for pension fund failures, has acquired more equities to try to reduce its own deficit[43].

Valuation of the asset side of pension funds is, in accounting terms, straightforward. The accountant simply asks for the market price at his chosen date. Future returns employ a degree of conjecture, justified only on the principle that the future is a straight line continuation of the past. We have already discussed economic cycles and long cycles, so any straight line projection will be dubious. But what about the liabilities, the pensions that must be paid for years? There are two factors: mortality rates and discount rates.

Accounting standards adopted at end 2005 provided scope for pension funds to take estimated future returns into account, making it harder to establish what liabilities businesses may have had to their pension funds. Accounting standards had previously allowed choice of mortality assumptions[44].

Discount rates are used to convert future values into the present day equivalent by recognising the time value of money. Unlike the fixed discount rate used by the Private Finance Initiative, pension fund liabilities are determined using corporate bond yields as a variable discount rate. The credit crisis has pushed these yields up in recognition of the higher risk that now attaches to corporate borrowing compared to government borrowing. In fixed interest markets, a move to higher yields brings lower prices and, for existing investors, capital losses.

This leads to a strange accounting result. Pension funds invest in corporate bonds. The higher yields that occurred in the credit crunch (because prices of corporate bonds had fallen) were used to discount liabilities and hence produce lower deficits[45].

Another example of assumptions regarding pension costs has appeared in the British government's plan to discount public sector pension liabilities at the inflation rate plus 3%, on the argument that 3% is the assumed rate of growth of the British economy and therefore of the tax base that will pay those pensions. This assumption has been criticised by accountants and actuaries as likely to understate the future cost of public sector pensions[46].

There is a much better way to measure financial risk in pension fund liabilities. It is to separate estimated future mortality rates from investment returns, disclosing both the mortality rate used and the effect of improved mortality rates on liabilities. Funding should be calculated based on a pure Gilt portfolio, one in which there is certainty of investment returns (which means leaving index-linked Gilts out). Then the actual funding can be compared to the Gilt based funding, which would lead to a measure showing the true investment risk. All the wishful thinking assumptions would then be shown for what they are: hostages to fortune[47].

The accounting profession has grown increasingly concerned about pensions and has proposed a number of changes[48]. Predictable howls of anguish have been heard[49]. If adopted, many pension funds will show severe deficits, as the wishful thinking implicit in bubble accounting will be revealed. The proposals include: using the risk-free yield on Gilts instead of the corporate bond yield as a discount rate for liabilities, requiring pension plans controlled by employers to be consolidated in the employers' accounts, preventing use of more optimistic assumptions for assets than for liabilities and using actual returns earned on assets rather than assumed future returns. Such changes will resolve the shortcomings I have identified, even though there would be a painful adjustment as reality replaces wishful thinking about pension liabilities.

The fashion for alternative assets

I found an advertisement on the Internet for *"The Alternative Investment Summit 2006."* "Why should you attend the Alternative Investment Summit? Pension Funds ... Evaluate the case for investment in hedge funds, private equity, commodities ..."[50]

One of the most basic rules of investment survival is to recognise that it is impossible for everyone to get rich by placing the same bet. The act of betting itself drives prices upwards, producing the illusion of continuing capital gains. Once the crowd turn tail and sell, prices tumble and the illusion is exposed.

The curious thing is that, as pension funds jumped on the hedge fund bandwagon, so hedge fund returns declined: their moment of greatest glory had passed. The reason, of course, is the old problem that when a certain type of investment is small and little known, returns are greatest, but when it is popular, the very scale of funds involved prohibits anything spectacular.

The big speculation of 2005 was commodities and in late November 2005 the *"Commodity Investment World Europe"* conference included topics such as: "Utilising commodities to boost your portfolio" and "The case for commodities[51]."

As in all previous speculations, commodities became a fashion with investors under pressure to conform by joining the party. Financial fashion always prospers when easy credit and greed are both in the ascendant. But conferences tend to come **after** everyone else has jumped on the bandwagon. Reports in the financial press in 2004 and 2005 showed that British occupational pension funds had about 8% of their assets in hedge funds and commodities, which was up from almost nothing five years earlier.

This was probably why the oil price went so high: first, investment banks invented complex financial products based on the price of oil; then they sold them to pension funds who adopted commodities as a 'new asset class'. Their inflow of cash simply drove up the oil price. When pension funds collectively decided that they had invested enough in oil, the market ran out of buyers and the price fell. Future pensioners will now stand the losses, in much the same way as people's savings paid for the extravagances of the dot-com era.

Many occupational pension schemes are already in deficit; the value of their investments is insufficient to pay the promised pensions. There are five interested parties in each pension fund, all with different points of view – the pension fund itself, the sponsoring company, the pensioner and (in Britain) the regulator and the lifeboat, which is a mechanism providing financial support in lieu of failed pension funds.

Each pension fund that is in deficit will need to solve the problem. The first option is to turn to its sponsoring company for more cash. The deficit is a debt owed by the sponsoring company. Assuming that the company says *"no more cash,"* the pension fund will be forced to try to make good the shortfall through its investment policy[52]. This is why some pension funds have been buying hedge funds and commodities; by using bubble accounting, they can **assume** higher returns than in anything else.

Some occupational pension schemes dwarf the trading activities of their sponsoring companies. A mature scheme in a business that has shrunk in size may well have pension fund liabilities several times the annual turnover of the company. However, there is another side to this. Since a deficit in a pension fund has to be shown as a debt owed by the sponsoring company, changes in the deficit significantly affect the book value of the sponsoring company.

Many, many years ago, I went on a factory tour. The factory had its own heap of coal used in its particular industry. I discovered that the coal was revalued for the balance sheet every year, by looking at it, guessing its dimensions and quality, and coming up with a number for value. I suspected (but could not prove) that the size of the heap of coal was being used to smooth the profit and loss account, by reducing the stock value slightly in a good year and increasing it slightly in a bad year. Both management and shareholders love nice steady improvements in profit.

Pension fund deficits have taken on the role of that heap of coal. Funds have been able to make any reasonable assumptions they like, so long as they are disclosed, and change them as they think fit[53] for:

- future performance of any type of investment;
- future rate of inflation;
- future growth of salaries;
- mortality rates.

In a survey that I read early in 2005, 75% of pension funds assumed they would earn between 7.5% p.a. and 8.25% p.a. on their equity investments, **for ever**[54]. The survey commented that, given high returns in 2004, companies ought to be reducing their expected returns for the future. This is because of the law of reversion to the mean, the principle that high returns one period are followed by lower returns the next. Instead of following this law, some companies were actually increasing their assumed returns, by up to 0.5% p.a. Investments allegedly capable of outstanding performance, such as derivatives investing in commodities or a high yielding tranche of credit derivatives, could improve the assumed return of the fund. Mature pension funds (as in Britain and America) either invest in leading equities (and therefore depend on the prosperity of global business), or gamble in 'alternative assets' whose value depends on fashion[55]. In general, there has been a little reduction in equity content and a corresponding increase in Gilt and corporate bond investment, but the dependence on equities and alternative assets is, in my opinion, still rather high.

Much attention has been given to the so-called lifeboat, the Pension Protection Fund, which has power to levy all occupational pension schemes so as to raise funds to pay pensions for schemes that fail. In the best traditions of the British way, prudently run schemes are penalised and are expected to bail out messes[56]. This is the standard British design for any financial compensation scheme: spread the cost around the relevant industry, as it arises. In contrast, the American approach builds up an insurance fund in advance of any claim. The American method will ensure that the United States suffers *less* than Britain as this financial crisis unfolds. The British method will hobble Britain's financial services industry and its occupational pensions sector for years to come[57].

In tandem with the belief that equity returns will improve, mortality rate estimates may not be cautious enough. In Britain, the Pensions Regulator wants to change this and both the CBI and

National Association of Pension Funds have expressed deep opposition, causing at least a rethink.

Target date funds

Target date funds will be constructed to provide a projected sum at an expected retirement age, based on the assumption that the longer the time period, the more should go into the stock market. What this concept does not do is take any account of the capital market cycle. At this stage of the cycle, with a great bear market unfolding, such funds can only lose money for the public. The British government thinks everyone should save for a pension and is intending to make this compulsory. The sums invested in personal pension accounts, which are to be introduced later this decade, will be too small to offset a great flow of institutional money out of equities. However, in a 'bear' market in which there are more sellers than buyers, share prices have to fall. One has to question: what is the point[58]?

Property

Property is always an emotive subject. In America and Eire it has already played a major role in the credit crunch. In Spain, empty apartments abound in the Costa del Sol. Britain has its own peculiarities.

There are structural differences between residential and commercial property markets, but there are also similarities. Both have in common the dream of ever-rising prices, widespread belief that property is a store of value, and the dependence of lenders on borrowers to service and repay their debt.

Both commercial and residential property markets react slowly to change. In the case of commercial property, only lease expiries force fundamental values (or lack of values) onto landlords. Residential market prices are determined by the diminishing supply of mortgage funds: less money to lend secured on houses means lower prices.

In Britain, commercial property prices rose not only because of easy bank lending but also through pension fund buying. Meanwhile, shops and offices have been closing but many of these closures do not show up in published statistics. Commercial property takes a long time to respond to the state of the economy. For example, going back to the last property recession in the early 1990s, commercial rents were still falling a couple of years after Britain left the Exchange Rate Mechanism. As with all declining capital markets, capital values fall first then income (rentals earned from tenants) falls later. In this sense, commercial property behaves like the stock market[59].

All through the inflationary years, prices rose, banks had money to lend and did so, with the result that there was always more property coming into the market. In a self-fulfilling prophecy, property prices seemed to be a one way bet. Up. When inflation nosedived in the 1980 to 1982 recession, the world moved into an era of positive real interest rates – nominal rates higher than inflation. The first effect of this change was that money in the bank compounded even faster, so banks rushed to lend more. Then the authorities opened the credit floodgates wide; following the 1987 crash, even more money was on offer.

As the credit crunch showed, easy credit brings a sting in its tail: debt that needs to be serviced and repaid[60]. Slowly, this debt burden has grown to be the dominant factor in pricing houses. Households spend a high proportion of their income on mortgages and in many cases depend on two incomes to keep afloat. Likewise, commercial landlords need tenants paying rents in order to pay their own interest.

The home-owning dream

Rising prices in the inflationary years led to many people believing that property could never go down. Since house prices react slowly to economic and demographic trends, changes take a long time to be noticed. I believe house prices have peaked in many countries and must now decline slowly. There will be local exceptions, such as the top end of the London market, which may stand out from the general trend for a few years. But deep down, a major change is under way.

It seems to me that there are four reality check factors combining to force this trend change. They are:

- mortgage availability;

- demographics;

- economic activity;

- market saturation.

Let's look a little closer at them.

Mortgage availability

One of the driving forces in Britain's fifty-year bull market in residential property was the willingness of banks and building societies to lend. Once government policy turned to promoting credit as a tool of economic management, financial institutions felt even more pressure to lend. And so there was always a buyer who could raise a little more and offer to pay more, leading to a spiral of rising prices.

Today, banks are not lending. Month after month, the statistics report low levels of new mortgages. Banks can clearly see that property lending is now somewhat risky. Also, home buyers themselves are reluctant to over commit. The result is a dearth of transactions.

It takes both buyers and sellers to make a market. Buyers without finance cannot buy. Sellers without enough work to pay their way, may be locked into negative equity. But home owners generally believe in the value of their property, and property sales can take some time. So prices react slowly to the lack of demand, while potential supply stays off the market.

As the market drifts, lenders become even choosier about their offers of mortgages and a period of decline sets in. This is the point that British residential property is approaching, some four years later than America and three years after Spain.

In the depths of the credit crunch, UK lending on residential property was supported with Bank of England finance to banks and building societies. This source of funds is now to be withdrawn, creating yet more financial pressure on the market.

Demographics

Property salesmen are quick to promote apparently rational reasons why more homes have to be built. Common arguments are that people are living longer, or that there are more smaller households. These arguments are suspect.

Property ownership goes in a lifetime cycle, from first purchase through various stages of family home, smaller home, retirement home, to a final sale or transfer to the next generation. Not every household participates in every stage: some stay in the same home for half a century, many more move employment and home frequently. Across the entire market, as a generality, all the trading up and down nets out. The market is driven primarily by first-time buyers and last-time sellers.

First-time buyers are now scarce. The demographic reason is the fall in the birth rate in the 1970s and 1980s. Combined with postponement of initial purchase because prices are unaffordable, this has led to a lack of demand at the start of the chain. The birth rate has now stabilised and risen a little, so the number of first-time buyers will eventually turn up, but not for about another fifteen years.

Last-time sellers occur when people move into old folks' homes, or die owning property. The problem here is that, on average across the whole market, the next generation already own their own home. Some may decide not to sell, keeping two homes. But unless every inheriting family does this, there will be extra supply into the market caused by those sales. Extra supply is a mechanical result of owner occupation crossing 50% on a rising trend a generation ago. It will persist for another whole generation. So for a quarter of a century or more, extra supply will feed into the market. This will inconveniently overlap with lack of demand from first-time buyers.

Even if banks were willingly lending, the combination of lack of first-time buyers and surplus supply of inherited property would be damaging to house prices. Put these together and it should be clear that prices can only trend downwards, slowly, for fifteen to twenty-five years.

Now let's return to the salesman's dream of smaller households and longer life spans. The shift to smaller households dates from the 1970s and 1980s. It is reversing as younger people choose to stay longer with parents. Longer life spans are irrelevant, because the same families simply occupy the same houses for longer: no new demand is created.

Demographics worked in favour of rising prices when Britain was changing from a nation of renters to a nation of home owners. Now demographics works in the opposite direction, aiding lower prices.

Immigration is another demographic factor. It does create demand, but it is net immigration after emigration that matters. Here again, there is a problem with the widely held view that immigrants need extra housing. Net immigration of households is actually a little less than the rate of new housebuilding. Figures also indicate that half of all immigrants leave again within five years. Official counts of emigrants, particularly where Brits have acquired second homes in Europe and gradually removed themselves from the UK, are not that accurate[61]. It seems that a side effect of the credit crunch has been that some British émigrés are returning from places such as Spain, and the flow of outward emigrants has declined, leaving net immigration apparently rising[62]. Since returning British émigrés will have generally lost money on property abroad, the net effect may well be deflationary – replacing a valuable house by a cheaper property via an intermission spent in Spain, or not buying at all but renting instead as a house in Spain fails to sell.

The link between economic activity and residential property

Despite figures of economic growth, the British economy has not fully recovered from the credit crunch. The evidence is in chapter 6 but here I want to explore the link between economic activity and property.

Since incomes are under pressure and more job losses probably lie ahead, it is inevitable that some households will struggle to pay their mortgages. This will lead to arrears and repossessions rising slowly for some time. At September 2010, 1.55% of British mortgages had arrears exceeding 2½% of the total balance, and roughly 9,000 properties were being repossessed each quarter. These statistics were presented as an improvement[63].

At this rate, almost one in twelve mortgages will end in repossession over a typical twenty-five-year term. Far from being trivial, this is a serious social problem in the making. As austerity rolls on, the repossession rate is likely to rise, bringing the home ownership dream to an end for a significant proportion of households. Even at the present rate, nearly 900,000 households will face repossession over the next quarter century.

Repossessions in a falling market will result in financial losses as well as homelessness. The hapless owner, or former owner, loses any equity when prices fall. In Britain, mortgages bring a particularly nasty trap. Mortgage indemnity insurance usually advances funds to the lender, passing the recovery task from lender to insurer to recoup from the former owner. As a result, the borrower who cannot keep up with payments may lose his or her home and still have to pay off the lender. When former homeowners cannot pay, then the losses will fall on insurers or (depending on the extent of insurance cover) on the original lenders. Here the same barrier appears as with all debt forgiveness programmes: someone has to take real losses. If those losses are significant, then they affect lenders.

The British residential property market is now stagnant, with a low level of transactions owing partly to lack of mortgage availability. With the economy even chugging along – never mind another recession – prices will continue to decline, accentuating the downward spiral.

Lack of transactions means that people cannot move when they need to. Moves to new jobs become harder. Trading down to cut financial risk and costs becomes harder. And so the stagnant conditions in residential property feed back into the economy, contributing to the general malaise.

Market saturation

When a new market opens up, there is a period of growth as a product is widely adopted. Eventually everyone owns the product and demand falls away, turning into repair and replacement. This is the classic product life cycle. Think of consumer goods such as refrigerators, record players, mobile phones. In some cases (record players are an example) a new product (music downloads from the Internet) takes over almost completely.

Although changing very slowly, the residential property market is also subject to some of these life cycle factors. With owner occupation now at 71% of households, the great conversion from a nation of renters to a nation of owners is over.

Conversion flow (which we will examine further in chapter 8) drove the British property market for much of the last half century. Without it, only demographics and finance can affect prices. As I have shown, both of these are now negatives, which lead to a tortuous decline.

The financial case for borrowing to buy property was always that someone else would buy from you at a higher price. Thus borrowing geared up the return on a homeowners' equity. In the changed environment, borrowing is highly undesirable, since it works in reverse to destroy savings. Residential property is a roof over your head, but since prices can no longer rise, it is neither an investment nor a good store of value for the future.

Unique factors in the United Kingdom

The factors we have already explored are common in many

countries. The credit crunch was widely perceived as starting with American sub-prime defaults: the American residential property market now leads the world in showing how intractable these factors are.

Britain has some extra facets of the property problem:

◆ the difficult position of the younger generation;

◆ buy-to-let;

◆ existing self-certificated mortgages;

◆ mortgage equity withdrawal.

The younger generation has been priced out of home ownership. The strains show in family pressures, lack of labour market flexibility, and a deep divide between the lucky ones who inherit and the rest. Pricing young people into the market will be a desirable result, but it can only be achieved through existing home-owners facing losses.

Buy-to-let was a fashionable investment in the false boom years prior to the credit crunch. Investors who had burnt their fingers in the dot-com affair turned to property, aided by lenders flush with money. Now some buy-to-let investors also have to face losses. This is an inevitable result of being part of the crowd moving the market.

Self-certification enabled people to obtain mortgages without proving they could afford the debt. While regulators and lenders have clamped down on new self-certificated mortgages, there is an overhang of existing borrowers who either lack sufficient income, or may not be able to re-mortgage at the end of a fixed-term offer.

Mortgage equity withdrawal was another factor aiding the boom. Instead of trading down to a smaller property, it also took the form of borrowing. It seems to me that some of the supposed growth in the British economy came from increased borrowing on property, which was then spent on consumption[64].

The British residential property market is now built on over £1,100 billion of lending[65]. The earlier peak borrowing years of the late 1980s culminating in high repayment years from roughly 2010 to 2020 – into the second decade of this new millennium, will overlap with the much slower fall out from the latest property bust. These will be years of high capital repayment, of paying down debt rather than creating it. There will be a constant flow of capital out of stock markets to feed maturing endowment policies that were bought to pay off mortgage debt, with no matching inflows. This second property bust will take longer to correct itself. Far too many people have staked their financial futures on property investment, often using borrowed money. The deflationary effect of house prices that decline slowly for years and years has yet to be seen. Intermediate rallies, lasting more than a year before a renewed downturn appears, just serve to confuse both public and punditry alike.

Fashions fade through a series of independent steps, not just because of one single defining event. There will be horror stories emerging about people with heavy borrowings becoming forced property sellers into a weak market. Some of these forced sellers may be pension funds that have invested in property. So far as British residential property is concerned, the familiar story of bursting bubbles must return.

Other countries

American residential property has been yet another bubble. Sub-prime burst first and is therefore ingrained on the popular consciousness as the starting point of the credit crunch. But the earlier expansion of American lending occurred hand in hand with the British boom in mortgage lending. Both were overdue to go 'pop'. And it was the Brits (aided by Germans and others), not the locals, who were pushing holiday home prices up in Southern Europe, notably Spain, where the local bubble has also burst.

The Irish Republic was an extreme case of an economy built on property debt. Banks lent on anything that could be built, taking large bets on development projects. Anglo-Irish Bank alone lent about twice the Republic's total national debt. According to a report[66], Irish economists believed that worse conditions were yet to come, supporting the case that austerity without devaluation appears to deepen the downturn.

Given the significance of the American, British, Spanish and Irish property busts, it seems that property now has to affect the global economy.

The world's deficit with itself

America runs a current account deficit and pundits have encouraged the belief that America will need to devalue the dollar so as to reduce it.

The real issues are almost the opposite:

- ◆ America's deficit is the world's problem because the dollar is still the principal world reserve currency.

- ◆ America's deficit is nothing special. Other countries have proportionately far *worse* deficits.

- ◆ The world apparently runs a deficit with itself!

There is a basic accounting principle at stake here. Every surplus must be matched by a deficit because every cash flow across currency zone borders must be equal and opposite when looked at from both sides. The sum of all surpluses and deficits will therefore be zero.

Unfortunately, the world is not too good at measuring its cash flows, as these statistics *(Table A, page 70)* for OECD countries show. I will come back to non-OECD countries later[67].

What are the possible causes of this global deficit?

One possible explanation concerns three key non-OECD countries, namely China, India and Russia, for whom reliable data about total deficits (as opposed to direct trade deficits) is absent. These three countries were only in surplus while their booms lasted. Although they may be a factor, I do not believe they adequately explain the scale of this global deficit.

	End 2000	End 2003	End 2006
Surplus countries	+$ 317 bn	+$ 348 bn	+$ 144 bn
Deficit countries	- $ 591 bn	- $ 699 bn	- $ 331 bn
Net deficit	- $ 273 bn	- $ 350 bn	- $ 187 bn
Deficit/surplus ratio	**-1.86**	**-2.01**	**-2.30**

Table A – The world's deficit with itself

Misreporting is another explanation: either the failure to capture all private investment in deficit areas, or failure to capture all trade flows across borders. But misreporting should cause random errors rather than a consistent pattern, so it is unlikely to be the entire cause.

Another possible explanation is the development of offshore financial structures that appear on nobody's balance sheet. Official statistics do not fully measure offshore banking. They simply measure cash, deposits and total assets of banks. Total assets are, of course, mostly loans. Many of the Special Investment Vehicles that came to light as the sub-prime crisis progressed were 'off balance sheet'. Nobody can possibly know the extent of these financial hideaways. Many of the offshore financial structures are outside the statistics of their currency (and therefore country) of origin. Is it possible that they constitute another explanation for the misleading statistics concerning the US dollar and its deficit? This is the 'nobody knows' economy – it is measured in parts rather than misreported.

Finally, the black economy, that is, the flow of drugs and stolen goods, will also limit the accuracy of statistics gathered[68].

Inadequate data, misreporting, 'nobody knows' and the black economy may amount to much the same size as the American deficit. The plausible explanation is that much of the world's deficit with itself is really American in origin (because of the role of the dollar) and so the *true* American deficit may be almost non-existent. **This is how meaningless economic statistics can be.**

I also want to put the stated deficits – which may or may not be actual deficits – into perspective. *Table B* shows the figures for the 16 OECD countries that reported deficits at end 2006. Most of the data has been taken from the OECD statistics database, but there are inevitably some approximations and adjustments, particularly where I have had to convert reported data into US dollars. Although these 16 countries were in deficit, the other 14 OECD countries were in surplus.

Ranking by population *(Table C)*, the American deficit is only seventh in order of seriousness – and the warning signs were evident for Iceland.

Ranking by reverse size of the economy *(Table D)*, America's deficit ranks only tenth. Prior to the credit crunch, nobody suggested that Iceland, Hungary, Greece, Portugal, New Zealand, Spain, the Czech Republic, Australia and Turkey should devalue their currencies so as to solve their deficits. Now Iceland has devalued, and Greece may yet leave the Euro. Until the Euro breaks up, Euro members cannot devalue. So why pick on America?

Country	Deficit $ bn	Population m	GDP $ bn
USA	196	301	13,750
Spain	31	40	1,153
UK	25	61	2,472
Australia	14	20	687.9
Italy	13	58	1,862
France	12	64	2,244
Greece	9	11	238
Hungary	8	10	118
Turkey	6	71	389
Portugal	5	11	184
Czech Republic	3	10	129
New Zealand	3	4	104
Poland	3	38	418
Ireland	2	4	220
Iceland	1	0.3	14
Slovak Republic	1	5	53

Table B – The 16 OECD deficit countries at the end of 2006

Country	Deficit $ per person	Country	Deficit $ per person
Iceland	4,300	UK	408
Greece	840	Ireland	373
Hungary	839	Czech Republic	281
Spain	763	Italy	228
New Zealand	685	France	196
Australia	667	Slovak Republic	128
USA	650	Turkey	86
Portugal	489	Poland	68

Table C – The 16 OECD deficit countries at the end of 2006, ranked by population

Country	1000 * deficit GDP	Country	1000 * deficit GDP
Iceland	89.0	Turkey	15.8
Hungary	70.9	USA	14.2
Greece	37.8	Slovak Republic	13.0
Portugal	28.1	UK	10.0
New Zealand	27.0	Poland	8.7
Spain	26.7	Italy	7.1
Czech Republic	22.3	Ireland	7.0
Australia	19.8	France	5.6

Table D – The 16 OECD deficit countries at the end of 2006, ranked by GDP

Table C and *Table D* show that Iceland's collapse was overdue, a point that nobody noticed at the time. They also show the warning flags for Greece and Hungary.

There is another comparison that can be made, between the deficit on a GDP basis and the extent to which a currency is over- or undervalued against the dollar, for which *The Economist's* Big Mac index is the easiest comparator to use. Only the extreme adjustments matter: when I originally researched this, Poland was 40% undervalued (so Poland moves up); Iceland 114% overvalued (so Iceland had to move down, as it has now done)[69].

This brings me to the role of the dollar. The dollar remains the dominant currency in the world, the one that people run to for safety, and the currency that prospers in a global downturn. The Euro failed to supplant this role in the good times and cannot do so now it is under pressure. It may be that in another half century the Renminbi or the Yen will become prominent, but first China has to go through the inevitable bust of a newly emergent nation[70] and Japan has to face up to its seriously insolvent banks. Neither country is anywhere near achieving a world reserve currency role. Since the dollar is the world's money, people need to hold dollars to trade. This role is not going to disappear for some years.

As I have shown, America's deficit is nothing special. The case for the United States being in severe deficit seems to be largely a construct of inadequate statistics and insufficient analysis. Proportionately, other countries have a far worse problem.

There is much talk about how currencies are determined by economic trends, with little evidence to support this. The three most important factors seem to be:

◆ prospective real yields – because money flows to where it can earn most[71];

◆ monetary policy (which is linked to real yields), because creating much more of currency A than currency B, must result in the price of currency A falling against currency B;

◆ sentiment – the irrational behaviour of market participants that allows over and under valuations to appear as market players follow the short-term trend. This is particularly true of the carry trade, which distorts relationships while the fashion lasts.

Sentiment ran against the dollar during the great credit boom of 2003 to 2007 and is now reversing with each flight to quality. Monetary policy also depends on differences: the Bank of England and the European Central Bank may have their political briefs changed as recession unfolds. Prospective real yields will change naturally because as recession deepens, inflation rates fall away.

All exchange rates are relative. For Britain, Sterling will continue to weaken as the statistics show deterioration in the UK economy. The dollar is still the ultimate haven currency. As deflation comes back into the news and risks from bad debts rise, the dollar will again become the currency of choice.

Devaluing the dollar

Devaluing the dollar shrinks the world monetary base since about 70% of world assets are dollar denominated. If the monetary base shrinks, then banks have fewer deposits as a base for their lending, so the credit supply will then shrink. The risk of declining bank lending is now recognised. Devaluing the dollar simply adds to the downward spiral in lending.

Thus, devaluing the dollar makes the world's existing financial problems worse rather than better. This does not quite square up with the notion that America's current account deficit needs to be eliminated. The explanation is that America's financial problems belong to us all, simply because the dollar is the dominant world currency.

Twin design flaws in the Euro

Europe already suffers from inadequate economic growth. A stronger Euro can only increase the recessionary forces in Europe. There is tension between Germany (seeking to avoid inflation) and France (seeking to buy growth at almost any price). There is tension between the core of Germany and France, compared to the fringe of Greece, Portugal and Ireland. There has been talk of Greece being forced out, and even Germany leaving so as to protect its own industry.

Deep down, the Euro has two design flaws. The obvious one is that there is a central bank but no central Treasury, so monetary policy is centralised yet each member sets its own fiscal (taxation) policy. Bureaucratic design ignored the lesson of history, that political union and a central Treasury have to precede currency union.

The Greek crisis showed once more that politicians always put bailouts first. This is where the second design flaw comes into play. The European Central Bank allows all commercial banks in the Euro-zone to borrow at a preferential rate if they deposit sufficient high-grade collateral, namely government debt securities. The preferential borrowing rate is 1%. This allows banks to deposit some security, take the cash and reinvest it in further government bonds earning 3% to 6%. It's another official scheme creating credit, with only the system limit to restrain it. Let it continue and the strains in the Euro will deepen; end it and Euro-zone economies must decline[72].

A thousand years ago, Britons learned the lesson that natural forces always win[73]. Markets are akin to natural forces: they cannot be suppressed by rules and regulations[74]. The only issues that matter for the Euro are just how and when it will crack, and which European politicians will be blamed for their grand failure of bureaucratic design.

Debtor and creditor nations

It is often argued that the United States has turned into a gigantic debtor nation, dependent on the creditor nations of the East to support it financially. The worry is that China and other Eastern nations will cease to support the United States, leading to a collapse in the US Treasury bond market and a further drop in the dollar. Japan has failed to lead the world since its own great deflation set in[75]. Instead, China emerged from the shadows to become a major economic force.

China is in a classic transition from an agricultural economy to a manufacturing economy. Nations that become major players on the world stage always make such a transition: Britain did so in the Industrial Revolution, America as it exploited the motor car. In achieving 'workshop of the world' status, any nation acquires a strong currency and a surplus of savings. As a result of its one-party State, however, China is able to do what more democratic nations find difficult, namely concentrate on what is good for China. It is notable that China has been expanding rapidly, putting Chinese interests first at every opportunity. Authoritarian governments can do this if they are commercially minded.

China needs to reinvest its surplus, which to some extent it does in US Treasury bonds. However, in assuming that this is a factor explaining low interest rates, there is a degree of confusion about cause and effect. Many central banks have forced interest rates down and pumped credit furiously. In a world already pressured by its cumulative debt burden, this has given the appearance of growth. This increased credit supply enabled western consumers to spend more on imported goods and China rose to the challenge.

Japan could not do so, since it was already stuck in a prolonged deflation caused by its existing debt levels.

Credit growth in the US provided the fuel for China's growth. This is somewhat different from the view that China's growth caused western decline. Prosperity in the East has arisen directly from America's willingness to finance the world through its deficits. Had America followed a strong dollar policy throughout the credit interlude, China would probably not have industrialised on the scale it has. America's deficits enabled the rest of the world to prosper; they did not result from the rest of the world booming. The imbalances, surpluses and savings gluts follow directly from US monetary expansion.

International finance is certainly unstable. The instability arises from the world living beyond its means, financed by America's deficits and disseminated by investment banks. Apart from Japan, the nations of the East have no recent experience of recession. The slump in China's stock markets in 2007 and 2008 is a very big warning signal. For broader reasons, that we will cover in chapter 8, the subsequent rally was a selling opportunity.

5 Contradictions and paradoxes

The system limit explains the furious debate between those demanding further stimulus and those arguing for cuts. Each camp argues its own cause bringing consequences; the objections each makes to the other side's arguments highlight the short-comings of both. The contradiction was expressed clearly in a letter to the *Financial Times*[76]: "Do we have any science at all to stand on or is it just competing prejudice and opinion[77]?"

This chapter will examine the main contradictions and paradoxes. We shall return to the detail of the academic debate between economists in chapter 7.

Rescues and bailouts are self-defeating

On paper, governments have part nationalised many banks. You would think, therefore, that governments control banks. Where is the evidence? Apart from taxing bonuses, I see little.

If you are a banker and your bank is likely to go bust, taking the public's savings with it, it seems that governments will do anything to keep you afloat. The banks have been given pretty well everything they have asked for. Normal disciplines of the market economy – failing businesses are put down – do not apply. Banks are too large and too complex for our good[78]. Little discipline has been imposed on how banks treat their customers. Investment products that cannot possibly work in these turbulent markets are foisted on the public with complete disregard for the damage they may do[79].

Let's summarise what has happened to the bailout money:

1. Some has gone to restore banks' capital accounts, paying for bad debts.

2. Some went into financial speculation, notably via Exchange Traded Funds. The growth in commodity based Exchange Traded Funds may have fuelled inflation.

3. Some was lent back to central banks, preventing the stimulus from working.

4. Some went into real lending, though with consumers paying back debt faster than they borrow, it is difficult to see that much could have seeped through into real economic activity. At best, the rate of decline has slowed.

On this evidence, there is no case for more bailouts. But to understand why the system limit stymies rescues and bailouts, we have to undertake a 'what if?' exercise. What if governments succeeded in creating more credit, getting banks to lend it on to businesses and consumers? Could there indeed be a miraculous recovery in manufacturing[80]? What *would* happen next?

For governments to set the wheels turning again, debt levels would need to rise. However, few can afford the ongoing cost of more debt service and since total borrowing is already up against the system limit, it follows that insolvencies, arrears and repossessions would then rise.

After the Lehman débâcle, the threat that economic and therefore political destruction would be inevitable if public funds were lacking enabled some banks to restart the speculative game profitably, even repaying some public money. Now the risks are rising as financial speculation increases.

The political systems in both America and Britain encourage governments to adopt short-term expediency. There is always an election on the horizon. Voters buy images rather than thought. Announce your policies before an election and you may lose votes from those who don't understand them or just disagree with them. The short-term natures of spin and quick initiatives are in complete opposition to the need to build skills and infrastructure for the future.

The ultimate short-term solution arrives when bank failure threatens. Bank failures are disastrous. Workers' wages do not get paid; savings are lost; pensions disappear. The pressure to rescue the system is always greater than the need for a rational long-term plan. Policy has always been that failing banks should be bailed out. Each bailout has led to further speculation then, a year or two later, another crisis erupts. The overall result of a policy of injecting more spending power, i.e. credit, and bailing out the system is that bigger crises come round faster.

Buying off every threatened bank failure does more than create another crisis to follow. Most of the bank failures experienced so far have been liquidity failures, that is, lack of cash. Further bailouts will cause rising bad debts, eventually bringing solvency failures when bad debts overwhelm bank capital. The short-term fix is not just bringing another crisis around, but creating the worse one of solvency failure.

Again, the concept of the system limit helps understand why this should be so. In the 1930s, the world was not up against the system limit and therefore stimulating economies to keep spending going, at the price of future public sector debt, was a viable policy option. Now both public and private sectors are up against the system limit.

The ultimate stimulus is Quantitative Easing, printing money to buy government debt in the hope that some gold dust will fall on the broader economy through lower yields generally. All this does is continue the policy started by Dr Greenspan. There has been concern that a law of diminishing returns has set in, with successive rounds of stimulus having less effect. Quantitative Easing attempts to perpetuate the myth that governments can find policy options to fix the economy. The system limit thwarts the policy.

The austerity contradiction

Since the bailouts that eased the credit crunch, policy has reversed to cut expenditure until savings can reduce public debt. This puts the cycle into reverse gear. Cutting expenditure cuts economic activity, which means that more households and businesses find themselves struggling to service their existing debt burden. As more cuts follow, a downward trend develops.

The pensions shortfall will then add to the downward forces. Shortfalls in pension schemes can only result in lower income and purchasing power for pensioners. Pensions will reinforce the economic decline.

Financial upsets are inevitable once debt becomes unaffordable. Banks are asked, as a matter of policy, to hold more capital in the belief that this will strengthen the financial system. But they then have less to lend, which weakens the financial system, again reinforcing the downward cycle.

Culling the public sector, the quango State and the vast overheads imposed by secondary and tertiary legislation ought to provide an alternative to higher taxes or cutting front-line services, but it will bring the public sector into deliberate austerity. How will all those displaced quangocrats pay their mortgages?

This is the austerity contradiction. Austerity brings a new set of problems. So far as Britain is concerned, rising mortgage arrears will collide with rising taxes to produce a new wave of social misery: the real price of the credit boom may well be a homelessness crisis.

Declining economic activity means that government will find its tax revenues falling just as benefit claims rise, so it puts tax rates up and cuts social benefits to try to balance its books. Inevitably, lower benefits and higher taxes will again limit economic activity. Plus, in a competitive world, higher taxes can only drive the successful out of the UK.

Canada and Sweden are often quoted as examples of beneficial austerity policies. But when those countries successfully adopted austerity, the rest of the world was still booming. Britain's adoption of austerity comes against an incipient global downturn. The background has changed; the examples of Canada and Sweden are less relevant.

An economy in which a certain growth in debt creates a bigger growth in the economy is basically healthy. But one in which growth in debt has exceeded growth in the economy is anything but healthy: it is fundamentally unstable. With one hand the British government is trying to reduce its debt by austerity. At the same time, the other hand is trying to increase private sector debt using Quantitative Easing. In combination, these policies replace an indebted State by making its citizens excessively indebted instead.

When economic relationships change

University economists have sought to explain how the economy works through extensive use of computer models. Starting from the mechanical model on view at Cambridge (the Phillips machine), the scope of models has expanded roughly in line with the computing power available. The problem is that economic relationships do not stay constant, they vary with the long run cycle.

I believe two fundamental changes have occurred in recent years. The first is a direct result of the credit crunch: personal borrowing being replaced by financial rectitude. The second is a mechanical result of the way trends cause relationships to change when a 50% threshold is crossed. Let's examine each.

Changed behaviour

People are now less keen to acquire debt and more willing to pay debt down. Those households and businesses desperate to keep borrowing are unlikely to be supported by banks, because they are bad risks. Others who do not borrow are hardly going to volunteer to do so in order to support the financial system. Falling levels of consumer borrowing presage lower economic activity. Businesses will be squeezed from both directions, lack of finance and lack of demand, causing business activity to slow down. This squeeze can only be deflationary. It is impossible to have lasting inflation without continually expanding bank lending and consumer borrowing.

The 50% factor and the savings contradiction

Now what happens to a nice predictable relationship between economic variables when it crosses the 50% level? Traditional economic relationships work differently once this level is exceeded.

Take, as an example, residential property in Britain. I noted the change brought about by crossing the 50% home ownership barrier on a rising trend a generation ago in the previous chapter: there is a mechanical drag on the market starting a generation after the 50% threshold was crossed, lasting for another generation.

The point that matters here is the significance of this change at 50%. All Western economies are now devoted to consumption and services. Manufacturing accounts for only 13% of the British economy (measured as GDP) and 10% of British employment. Over 50% of British economic activity is consumption. During all the years of rising consumer spending, economic prosperity and increased consumption were handmaidens. Now, as consumers cut back, the economy turns down. The old theory that saving led to investment, which in turn led to more production and more growth, has gone. In its place, saving more individually (which is the same as paying down debt) leads to collective misery. An economy in which over 50% of economic activity is consumption, is peculiarly vulnerable to this change in consumer behaviour.

Growth or decline?

Economic theory says that money spent on capital goods for the purpose of trade is investment. The trade will, hopefully, earn a profit and investors will receive an income from their capital. The two most common forms of capital structure are fixed interest and equity. To raise fixed interest capital, the business sells a loan stock on which it pays the investor interest. Equity investors expect a share of profit paid as a dividend. If a company has both types of capital then fixed interest must usually be paid before any dividends.

The theory was developed in the industrial revolution, driven by manufacturing. Today, manufacturing has decamped to countries such as China and both Britain and America have relatively small manufacturing industries. In both countries, something like two-thirds of economic activity is accounted for by consumer spending. Manufacturing economies were financed by savings, but when an economy is based on consumer spending, growth is financed by expanding household borrowing which promotes more spending. Nobody noticed as consumption became the dominant part of the economy, because it seemed that economies were powering ahead; the connection to growth in debt was not understood[81].

Economic theory also describes the relationship between the level of a currency and inflation. When Britain was in the Exchange Rate Mechanism (ERM), all the opinion-formers agreed that devaluation would cause inflation. Black Wednesday sent the pound down and yet little inflation was observed. The inflation rate was 10% when Britain joined the ERM and has never been back to that level[82]. Likewise, in recent years, America has tried devaluing the dollar, with little effect on inflation. The growth of China as a low cost manufacturing country has also insulated us from the traditional higher cost of imports. Just like the theory that saving leads to investment, the theory that devaluation leads to inflation is obsolescent.

China is mostly dependent on the West for its industrial success. Reducing Western demand, through a prolonged consumer-led downturn, will burst China's bubble. This is probably why the Chinese stock markets have already been so erratic. Changing one set of economic policies always has consequential effects; changes in economic conditions in one country cause knock-on effects elsewhere. The system limit of debt keeps reappearing as a brake on any solution. Growth in the total supply of money is failing to create either economic growth or even sufficient inflation. Living standards were already declining long before the credit crunch appeared in the headlines. Yet some of the money the authorities have provided did get through the system. It went into commodity and food price inflation!

We are led to believe that there is no cost to the public purse in extensive bailouts, since central banks can create money. But there is a delayed cost, which itself is poorly appreciated. Central banks are taking collateral for their loans to the banking system. This collateral may well be triple-A low risk debt, but the sub-prime crisis showed how quickly bad debts can spread. Central banks are not immune to such bad debts. Some high quality collateral today will become bad debt when recession deepens tomorrow. But taxpayers cannot afford unlimited support to the banking system and their reluctance to pay ever higher taxes will soon appear. While the good times rolled, higher taxes were seen as a mark of success and accepted. Now one must question: at what level is an economy damaged by taxation? Clearly if we spent 100% of income on taxes, we would live on government food parcels in public housing and have no pocket money. At what level does Britain cease to have a functioning competitive economy? 75% of income spent on taxes? 50%? Perhaps a publicly funded university would like to investigate?

When growth is decline: distinguishing economic growth from credit and regulatory growth

In chapter 3 we saw how growth in credit in Britain had been three times the rate of economic growth plus inflation, and therefore the growth of debt had been counter-productive. Statistics of growth adjusted for increased debt, or growth adjusted for increased overhead, are conspicuous by their absence: both would probably show severe negatives, to the embarrassment of many governments. In Britain's case, simply deducting credit growth from reported economic growth would result in a relative decline of between 6% and 9% annually according to how inflation is accounted for.

There has been a completely artificial credit-induced expansion of

Western economies, promoted by politicians who would rather you only looked at the asset side of the balance sheet while ignoring the liabilities, namely the debt used to create it. It has been accepted practice to consider only one side of the economic use of credit. If a business said "profit = revenue" ignoring all expenditure, or "net worth = assets" ignoring all liabilities, it would be shut down as fraudulent. I find it hard to see the difference for economic statistics that ignore debt. This misrepresentation of the causes of growth is endemic throughout Western economies. Economic growth should be more than the debt used to finance it, yet it has been only a sorry fraction of that rise in the debt burden. This deceit needs to come to an end. The contradictions of public policy need to be aired and difficult choices made. The basis for all past economic policy choices was credit creation, but Keynesian solutions cannot work because credit creation no longer works.

Debt growth is only one side of this contradiction. Overheads have been rising steadily. To the average indebted household, interest is an overhead cost. These costs have been rising across the economy, yet nobody has quite understood how.

From figures released by the Economic Research Council, we do know that the cost of the British bureaucracy exploded from £24 billion to £167 billion annually in just eight years. The money spent on bureaucracy now accounts for five times the defence budget[83]. The total growth of GDP over the same time was £368 billion, so it follows that 45% of our economic growth has been spent on the overhead activities of regulation and compliance, not on productive economic effort at all.

Mortgage equity withdrawal contributed up to £161 bn to economic growth in 3½ years[64]. Prior to the credit crunch, most of Britain's growth was either borrowed for consumption, or added to overheads by regulation. Living standards did not really rise. People were already working harder to finance their personal debts before recession arrived, while at the same time unproductive bureaucratic overhead creation was in progress.

Businesses pour effort into compliance because of endless regulation. Expanded private sector effort in compliance is measured as productive economic growth and therefore counts in the growth statistics. Compliance in public sector organisations is also soaking up money, but is counted as 'productive' growth in public sector spending. This may help to explain why front-line services seem so stretched and there is so little to show for all the public spending of recent years. It also explains why business is so desperately price competitive. Anyone who believed the growth propaganda will now learn a very hard lesson.

Government mandated spending

Public spending is an area that has caused increasing concern recently. I believe it is only part of the problem. What matters is government mandated spending. We have already noted that the costs of regulation and compliance form an overhead activity, erroneously measured as growth. Financial services was just the pioneer of this. The overhead activities of our society consist of the sum of public spending AND the private sector spending that is mandated by government. Nobody has thought about it, but with public spending running at around 50% of GDP, I would hazard a guess that total government spending plus mandated spending on the orders of government, forms somewhere between 60% and 75% of GDP[84]. Real economic activity must have been shrinking while this explosion in overheads has occurred.

Although there are figures for public spending and public sector debt, a true test of State influence would include all private sector activity carried out at State direction. Quangos that are funded by user charges on industry? They clearly fall within the realm of State direction. Costs borne by businesses in satisfying compliance requirements? They too are State imposed. Time spent by citizens in satisfying the great bureaucracy? This also is required by the State.

In a competitive market economy, the State feeds off entrepreneurial activity but does not weigh it down and the private sector should account for over half of Gross Domestic Product even after making allowance for the economic costs of quangos and compliance tasks. This is no longer true in Britain. While the credit supply was growing and we enjoyed the illusion of prosperity, the true cost of State direction was ignored.

Britain does not have a competitive market economy. The dominant economic force in Britain is the combination of government mandated spending plus public expenditure. The quango State is one set of overheads, but the cumulative weight of government requirements imposed on business also affects competitiveness.

Financially, Britain is a mess caused by its excessive debt burden and inflated property prices. Structurally, Britain is a mess caused by excessive reliance on financial services and retailing. As a nation, Britain is a mess caused by excessive prescriptive regulation[85] and its entitlement culture[86]. But the real economic issue to be tackled is getting aggregate State spending plus mandated State spending back below 50% of economic activity. Since State spending alone was 48% of GDP for 2009/10[87], Britain has much to do[88].

Government mandated spending extends State control to the majority of the economy, replacing the influence lost by privatisation, whereby government disposed of publicly-owned businesses by selling the public what they already collectively owned. As a revenue raising mechanism, selling the family heirlooms is over, yet government still controls the majority of the economy through its compliance requirements.

There are two further factors that extend State control over the private sector of the economy. They are substitute taxation, which raises extra revenue and substitutes for public ownership, which extend State influence. They are worth a deeper look.

Substitute taxation

Tax gathering in Britain used to be remarkably efficient. To generate its major revenues, government typically spent 1% of the sum raised[89]. Of course, this does not measure all the work done by employers, which is conveniently classified as productive economic effort, but that's another story.

Since the National Lottery started, many Britons have been paying what amounts to a new voluntary tax. Half of the money raised is spent on public causes; the other half (less costs) is returned to an arbitrarily selected few. As a gambling chip, this is slightly more effective than the stock market because a few more people succeed in making serious money. As a substitute for taxation, it is the most expensive and economically inefficient scheme ever devised. But it does have one tremendous advantage over most taxation. You can legitimately avoid the tax, cost free, by choosing not to participate.

Substitutes for public ownership

The Lottery tax gatherer is a Canadian owned business. My electricity supplier went American. The water industry seems to be going European. Rail freight has gone American. What makes Britain's ex-public sector so attractive?

The common factor linking the expensive tax gatherer and the foreign takeovers of recently privatised utilities, is the captive consumer who has to pay up. Businesses now thrive on public sector contracts where the consumer pays via user charges and penalties. The old name for this was tax farming. As a simple example, if the police recover a stolen car, they extract whatever evidence they can then hand it over to a contractor. The contractor arranges for victims to collect their cars, for which storage and recovery charges are levied. Consumers are forced into accepting costs imposed by government (or resulting from government action) that a truly competitive economy would never allow to happen.

The conflicts in easy answers

In pretending that overheads are growth, government misclassifies costs. If a business misclassified costs so as to pretend they were economic gains, it would be in some difficulty with audit. Yet government can misclassify on a grand scale and nobody raises an eyebrow. Nobody knows just how deep the effect of classifying overhead activities as productive economic growth goes. My guess is that it accounts for much of the total growth in the economy over the last dozen years. Like a bubble company, it has been an undertaking of apparently great advantage. But nobody knows exactly what it is.

We must learn not to expect easy answers from our politicians. There are no tricks that can present excess debt as a good thing for ever. Mortgaging the future, via PFI, can only give us a worse repayment burden, as in Greece. Governments are in more than a policy trap: they are in a financial trap as well. A combination of increasing lifespan, declining birth rate and early retirement, means that Western economies are all ageing. The shrinking economic pot has to be shared between progressively more people. That's hardly a formula for riches.

Official forecasts and the limits to government power

Britain's last serious recession, in which output fell, was in 1990 to 1992. Nobody under the age of 40 will now recall the run up to that recession. My starting point is the official story, though it is essential to realise that many of today's business leaders and most of today's political leaders had no experience of recession whatsoever prior to the credit crunch[90].

Back in 1988 and 1989, the official line was that the minor problem exhibited by stock markets in 1987 had been solved. There was some inflation, which governments were determined to fight by using higher interest rates. Britain shadowed the Deutsche Mark and then joined the Exchange Rate Mechanism. This deepened the recession which was already in its incipient stages. The same mistake of putting a hypothetical fight against inflation ahead of precautionary measures to prevent a recession was made then, as it was in the run-up to the credit crunch.

Before it became obvious that the economy was in trouble in 1990, the official line from the Treasury was that there would be continued growth thanks to the stability brought by the Exchange Rate Mechanism. Then the growth figures started slipping. The spin was that the economy was fundamentally sound. Pundits took the hint and talked about a 'technical recession', as if there was not really anything wrong beyond a meaningless artefact of the statistics. The Treasury continued forecasting that growth lay just around the corner, even as negative equity swelled and unemployment rose.

The escape route, of course, was to leave the Exchange Rate Mechanism, slash interest rates and let the currency go. This heralded another credit boom making the earlier post-1987 credit boom look puny. A third credit boom followed with the millennium, and a fourth to fix the dot-com crash.

There's some interesting evidence of the shortcomings of official forecasting in my press cutting library. Much of it will have been forgotten and therefore as a contribution to the forecasting profession, a summary of some key points from the 1990-1992 recession follows.

Treasury forecasting

In 1991, the *Sunday Times* published a careful analysis of political spin in economic statistics. David Smith, still its Economics Correspondent as I write this book, showed how both the then Conservative government and Labour opposition were manipulating statistics to suit their own ends[91].

Nine months later the same newspaper analysed successive Treasury forecasts in detail. It discovered that they were consistently wrong by serious amounts: economic growth had averaged 2.5% over the years, yet the Treasury's own forecasts had been wrong by 1.0%, up or down, which may sound small but is 40% of the average. The assumptions about people's behaviour, on which so much economic modelling was based, were themselves wrong[92].

This point, that the methods and assumptions were wrong, was developed by Brian Reading in the same issue of the *Sunday Times*. He noted that, paradoxically, false forecasts of an early recovery make matters worse. *The Economist* then went on to argue that accuracy in forecasting lies in diversity, rather than in consensus seeking[93]. The wider lesson was also forgotten as the boom of 2003 to 2006 proceeded: diversity needs to extend to opinion sources.

Finally, the *Financial Times* published a letter from the late Prof. Wynne Godley, then of the Department of Applied Economics at Cambridge, showing the Treasury forecasts from March 1990 to March 1992 compared with actual out-turn. During the period that Britain was actually diving into recession, the Treasury never once forecast that recession[94].

So my conclusion is: do not rely on official forecasts. When things go awry such forecasts will be utterly useless. In this vein, one has to observe that forecasts of an end to recession, of green shoots espied, or over-precise forecasts of how much economies will decline or recover in the next year or two, must be suspect.

Do governments have any power?

Day-to-day life in Britain is increasingly dominated by petty regulations. Take great care how you park your car in case you get a fine. Take great care what you put in your rubbish bin in case you get another fine. Take great care what you say to any official in case you get yet another fine. There are so many regulations, who has a clue what they all are?

All this control from on high should reinforce the message that government is all powerful. On the contrary, the market always wins. The market cannot be abolished even by European directive. When governments meddle with markets natural economic forces are blunted for a period of time, but return with renewed vigour later. Eurocrats please note.

We have lived through a credit bubble, evidenced by the gross borrowings of private equity funds and by excessive consumer debt. This credit bubble once served to convince people that economic management was sound and economic policy highly successful. But what price has been paid for this supposedly sound economic management? Let's think about how much we have literally mortgaged the future to pay for today:

- the average British citizen had total debts of some £23,000 to service *before* the credit crunch arrived and

97

government started borrowing more wildly[95];

◆ British businesses have been saddled with debt in the name of efficiency;

◆ hospitals and schools have been built on 30-year mortgages.

But there are two other sides to this story.

The first is that, to maintain apparent prosperity, people have to go on borrowing more and more. Only the act of spending borrowed money has kept economies afloat. Ah, goes the counter argument, but governments can always bail the financial system out with their power to print money. But someone, somewhere has to pay real interest on the instant money provided by each bailout. Given that banks are more choosy about lending and individuals less able to borrow, it should be obvious that every bailout providing new money must cease to have effect. The other sort of bailout, in which central banks swap debt (as offered by the Bank of England in spring 2008) is an attempt to get the taxpayer to pay for future bad debts arising from past lending. Since the lending in this particular example is on mortgages, the bad debts may continue for twenty-five years, to be paid out of future taxes. If this is not 'mortgaging the future', what is?

Many consumers are now stuck with unaffordable debt and they cannot afford to borrow more. Meanwhile, the British economy is burdened with thirty-year mortgages under the PFI banner, wasting resources for a whole generation. Those businesses given the private equity treatment of 'efficiency' are also saddled with excess debt. Here is the ultimate limit to government power: an over-indebted nation is crippled with debt service costs. Banks can only be forced to lend to businesses vulnerable to a recession by complete nationalisation and government control. Currently, banks are following their proper commercial judgment as to which businesses to lend to and which to decline. Interfering with this can only add to bad debts.

The link with evolution, delegated government and regulation

Our society divides policy into silos that barely understand one another and certainly do not communicate with one another. There is no common ground: for example, banks ignored prudential judgment about future bad debts because accounting standards specified detailed rules, rather than encouraging accountants to assess the dynamics and risks of the whole business. Accountants are not unique: many professions have replaced skill and judgment by codified requirements imposed on practitioners in the name of 'standards' or 'quality' or (in the public sector) 'targets'. Auditing accounts has become a matter of choosing which standards to apply, then checking that the standards have been followed. The standards are sacred[96].

The more rules that are made, the worse the problem becomes. Why? Because rules ossify the ruled and prevent evolution[97]. Unless the financial system delivers evolutionary change, the financial crisis can only turn into a political crisis. The more government outsources its responsibility for the economic health of the nation, the more delegated bodies there are to make their own sets of rules.

The same problems occur with taxation and with public expenditure. Taxation incurs dead-weight costs of administration, while public expenditure encourages unnecessary marginal use of scarce resources. Politicians are loathe to cut services but realise that rising taxes are unpopular. Public services, taxation, public borrowing and regulation are in a four-way contradiction: it is impossible to satisfy all four.

I showed earlier how the British economy was destroying value even before the credit crunch arose. Now the system limit ensures that any policy adopted makes matters worse. Doing nothing also allows the mess to compound naturally, just like compound interest. Hence radical thought is needed.

The political system limit

Changes to voting systems are but a trivial pursuit. The political system is also up against the system limit. Without change the crisis grows, yet every policy choice makes it worse. Britain has led the world in living beyond its means but the rest of the world is not far behind. Are we really a rich nation when so many owe so much? The credit excesses that built up in the twenty years following the 1987 crash were caused by politicians and central banks.

Sub-prime happened to be where the system limit first appeared, rather than the cause of the credit crunch. The entire world is set on a path to default. Predicting precisely where the defaults will come and when is as useless as trying to forecast where the credit crunch would break out and when. Default means debt needs to be written off and assets lost or confiscated to pay for it; it is the natural converse to the system that evolved from the early bankers to one in which no bank could possibly be allowed to fail. It is fairly clear that small profligate countries are seriously at risk. So are societies in which everyone owes everyone for the roof over their head. But to shrink the debt burden, a financial surplus must be generated. Resources have to be moved from monitoring and controlling, to productive creation of wealth. Future generations must be free to innovate, burdened neither by past profligacy, nor by stifling 'do it the prescribed way' regulation.

The problem is that British governments have been participating in wishful thinking on a grand scale, partly thanks to adversarial politics aimed more at point scoring and instant headlines than serious long-term thought. Aspirations were nurtured and a false prosperity created, as the whole western economy went on the biggest borrowing spree ever. A supporting cast of investment advisers, estate agents and loan brokers all grabbed the opportunity. It was a perfect example of the madness of popular delusions described by Charles Mackay[14]. The belief that house prices only rise, with the notion of riches to be gained through mortgage borrowing, even the refusal to countenance any other opinion, all faithfully follow the principles laid down by Gustave le Bon[98], which we will consider in chapter 6.

We now have to live with the consequences. Debt can only be serviced and repaid, or written off[99]. Money has been borrowed from the future and wasted. Later generations now face the burden of this folly.

Although Britain has extensive delegated public functions, local government has been neutered and simply recycles detailed rules laid down by departments of central government. Most State sector deliberation is behind the closed doors of unelected quangos, following prescriptive legislation from central government. In Britain, citizen participation is a farce of consultative groups with no power. No wonder people have lost faith in politics. How can we expect contemporary politicians to solve the problems caused by half a century of financial folly that previous generations of politicians have encouraged?

Why deflation is unavoidable

The underhand political alternative to bank rescues is to debauch the currency to try to inflate the way out, as in the Weimar Republic, or Zimbabwe. In such cases, hyper-inflationary excess causes economic collapse.

Today's problem is the other way round: economic collapse is coming first. This is deflationary: there is no money, so prices fall; the further lack of money then spreads through the economy. To turn this into inflation, either bankers must lend more to borrowers, or governments must print banknotes and give them freely to the public. The first method is clearly not going to happen *ad infinitum*. Lucky recipients of the second method would undoubtedly choose to repay their debt burden first: a one hundred fold expansion of the note supply would be needed to provide enough cash. The extra note supply would circulate from government direct to the public and back to the banks, with little additional spending and, therefore, no rise in price levels. In this environment, the act of paying down debt from artificial money does nothing for economic activity, nor does it cause inflation.

Any surge in the money supply initially causes the exchange rate to fall, thereby cutting consumer spending further, since consumerism and imports go together. These are the reasons why Quantitative Easing itself has limits.

It follows that price deflation is unavoidable. Falling asset prices must spread into falling spending, turning a short recession into a long drawn out decline, even if there are intermittent periods of apparent 'recovery'. Japan really does show us the way.

Global paradoxes

Now I want to bring some global paradoxes into consideration.

- ◆ Why are most pundits wrong about government debt?
- ◆ What are the broader paradoxes of capitalism?

Government bond markets

As I write this, the current worries are that some smaller European nations might default, or leave the Euro; and America may go into a double-dip recession. Earlier, Britain was in the centre of the default stories. By the time you read this, completely different stories will be in the headlines.

Take the defaulting governments story first. Thanks to the system limit, the whole world is in a financial pickle. In a country having control of its currency, the internal promises of governments are the safest guarantees in that country's financial system: the strain can be taken by devaluation. The extent to which an independent government can sell debt internally depends on the need for its guarantees. In a currency union, the strain has to be taken by unemployment and wage cuts (as in Ireland) or by exiting the union.

In the case of Britain, there is ample potential demand from pension funds, whose individual financial plight worsens as the greatest crash continues. There is further demand from banks, who will be forced to hold more capital by regulators. And a general flight to quality itself produces additional demand for Gilts. Why were most pundits wrong-footed by the failure of Gilts to collapse when the Bank of England ended its first Quantitative Easing programme? I suspect that they only considered Quantitative Easing in isolation, ignoring the wider changes brought by the system limit.

As the greatest crash proceeds, most of the world will be affected. Companies will cut dividends more; corporate bonds will become riskier. This explains why US Treasury bonds and the dollar both rise with every flight to quality.

I am always suspicious of supply and demand arguments. They sound convincing, yet rarely tell the whole story. The world is in a bull market for quality government debt. In any bull market, supply expands as prices rise. Rising prices always bring in more buyers, and only rising supply can satisfy them. This has been the experience of every upward price leg in government debt markets for the past thirty years.

Broader paradoxes of capitalism

The United Nations was founded with 51 members in 1945,

although some countries did not join until 1955/6. In 1946, there were about 74 independent States in the world; today there are 193[100]. As the old empires have declined, the world has fragmented into ever smaller units of organisation. And yet these States have been forming broader alliances: the EU, NATO, the North American Free Trade Area and so on. Will the broad alliances unify and merge, or will more units fragment?

Do we respect sovereignty and the rule of law, or intervene to protect human rights? Just like the contradictions of finance, so international policy contradictions are signs of the times. Iraq shows the case for recognising international paradoxes **before** rushing in. The public case for intervention was based on the false premise of Weapons of Mass Destruction. The human rights case was poorly thought through, with inevitable consequences years afterwards.

If you think the world is set for boundless prosperity based on the triumph of capitalism, I would suggest you think again. Consider, for example, Iraq and Iran, Afghanistan, Vietnam and Cambodia, China and Taiwan, India and Pakistan, Bosnia and Kosovo, Ethiopia Eritrea and Sudan, Korea, Russia, Japan, Mexico, Thailand, South Africa, Mozambique, Somalia, Chechnya, Chile, Indonesia, Northern Ireland, Burma, Yemen, Libya, Bahrain, Palestine, Algeria, Tunisia, Egypt, Syria and Britain's inner cities. Most of these demonstrate a similar combination of armed insurgency and economic decay. Then there are the nations and regions seeking American support, such as Latin America and Asia; and the interminable trade disputes.

Large business has moved from the 'multinationals' of 30 years ago to the 'global corporations' of today. But if you look at individual industries, you find exactly the same unification/fragmentation paradox. Almost every airline flies Boeing or Airbus, yet there are small airlines coming into existence and many disappearing. Telecommunications is turning into a global business, yet there are more and more specialist telecommunications companies. Ford bought up niche car manufacturers, yet kept them as individual entities, but half a century ago British Motor Corporation created meaningless radiator badges. All these global corporations are, paradoxically, trying to track the spending habits of consumers by using database marketing to individuals. I doubt if many of them have ever thought about the possibility that some of their customers may stop spending altogether.

Capitalism has moved from the free market model to regulated markets. Some of the regulated markets, such as utilities in the UK, have been highly profitable, since regulation has proved effective in restricting competition. That particular tide may turn. Yet new competition comes from new directions. Here is an example: Macedonia, only recently an independent nation, intends to set itself up as a free-trade centre with tax breaks and incentives. While I do not think that Macedonia will be the next Hong Kong, the point is that bureaucratic capitalism will face similar threats.

In this age of uniformity, mass media, the dumbing down of standards, the demand for everyone to have a 'fair' share, whatever that may be, the constant erosion of individual liberties and the blanket imposition of identikit rules in the names of harmon-isation or regulation, all these lead to a dull, grey sameness. The new orthodoxy is: some people cannot discriminate, therefore nobody should benefit. Yet somehow islands of originality do survive and prosper, simply by being different.

Communism, Islam and population change

Religion, as known in the West, is in decline. The Church of England stopped publishing attendance statistics on the grounds that its counting methodology was flawed. Communism has also, apparently, been in decline. Yet Kosovo showed a very strange religious alliance, the West and Russia aligned with Muslim interests against the Christian Communist Serbs. Something deeper is going on in the flow of ideas.

The European Union has expanded eastward with Poland leading the new members. At its heart, the European Union is driven by a bureaucracy attuned to the political, Statist drive of its major members. It is not a free-market economy in the sense that Americans would understand. I believe it is turning into an alliance of ex-capitalist nations and ex-Soviet dominated nations. It is the new Comecon, successor to the Communist era grouping.

One of the major trends to come is likely to be a merger between Communism and Islam, with a new Communislam offering salvation for those oppressed by debt. In such a world, business will be radically different and beyond most people's compre-hension. Anything to do with property or financial services will be changed beyond recognition. The scale of goods and services bought by end-consumers will be significantly reduced. This may be where evolution will take us.

When looking ahead there is no single right answer, only an ever-changing kaleidoscope of probabilities and possibilities. But there is one other factor we need to be aware of: demographics – the structure of population. Despite the hype that populations will grow, it is likely that world population will peak later this century and then shrink as the number of children born is less than the replacement rate needed to maintain the population. An ageing population will consume savings, yet savings are already under threat from ever lower yields.

If such a merger of Communism and Islam happens and then seriously impacts on global business, institutional investors will be locked into declining capital bases and declining dividend income. The oldest generation are, indirectly, dependent on the work and prosperity of younger generations. If the younger generations are absent, then all the numbers and regulations are useless: the value of existing savings must fall[101]. This is how the long-term trends interrelate.

6   Group think

Mass delusions and the media crowd

After the credit crunch started, many commentators referred to the absence of alternative view points during the period 2003 to summer 2007 as "Group think." There was a degree of hypocrisy about such comments, because the media were prime proponents of the story that Britain was booming. Viewpoints that this was completely false, and the credit merry-go-round would end in tears, were ignored. Only after a decent interval did some of the media admit that they knew of other views all along.

The story that Britain and the world had entered a new age of prosperity suited the Establishment. This rang true so long as the immediate, positive results of the debt spree were reported and the longer-term costs could be conveniently ignored. Of course, in an era of instant opinions, everyone believed the fiction, but it was nothing more than a mass delusion, propagated by a sympathetic media and aided by the Internet.

During the last decade, use of the Internet spread into every affluent household in the world. It has allowed popular view-points to be repeated *ad nauseam,* and thereby believed because of their repetition. A book appeared extolling the wisdom of crowds[102]. However, the defining work on crowd delusions and mass behaviour is *Psychology of Crowds* by Gustave le Bon[98], written late in the 19th century. Le Bon noted the importance of images in impressing the crowd, a lesson politicians still observe today. He also noted that repetition is used to make a story credible, a lesson duly copied by those politicians who blamed bankers for being the entire cause of the credit crunch. Above all, le Bon thought the crowd was a blockhead, reduced to simplistic judgments in complete unison. The crowd determines that it must be right; dissenters are ignored; gurus appear to tell the crowd exactly what it wants to hear.

Every financial mania in history has depended on two crowd delusions: the image of easy riches and repetition of the story. These are the facts behind every Ponzi scheme and every scheme that needs new money rolling in to pay the earlier investors. They are the rationale for investment managers offering to jump on every passing bandwagon, ignoring the problem that if they all jump off together, prices will crash. We shall return to how investors participate in manias in chapter 8.

As financial pressures have grown, the media have resorted to two kinds of differentiation: speedy response, and opinion/editorial pages. Let's look at how they both work.

News reporting has moved from legions of local journalists having time to get to grips with events, to rapid response accumulation of text messages, photos, emails and mobile phone calls. Some trade journals even use computer programs to cull news stories from websites without human intervention.

The quality media differentiate themselves by employing opinion writers. So far as business and finance are concerned, there is a remarkable tendency for every source to mimic what others are saying. Partly this is due to the pressure to produce copy quickly, sometimes in a few hours from brief to filing, and partly to the similarity of thought processes involved. Opinion-editorial writers themselves form a crowd, repeating the same stories uncritically. A classic example occurred early in 2010 when many British newspapers found reasons why Gilts were about to collapse in price, whereupon the Gilt market did the exact opposite and rose sharply.

There are a number of reasons why media opinions about markets are frequently wrong. The authors:

- forget that every opinion anyone holds anywhere is already "in the price," i.e. the market has discounted the story even before it is written;

- have little understanding of the concept of leading and lagging indicators, so that lagging indicators such as unemployment and repossessions are hailed when they turn down, even though the next upturn is inevitable, and leading indicators such as capital market movements are simply disregarded as "obviously wrong because you don't see the evidence around you";

- never consider the prospects for unpredicted change.

In 2008 the *Guardian* journalist Nick Davies, wrote a book that exposed shortcomings of the media[103]. He called it *Flat Earth News*; the core of the book was the evidence that newspapers and others endlessly repeat opinions as facts. Davies did not refer to le Bon, but he had rediscovered the same mass delusions.

Consensus or contrarian?

The consensus dictates how most people see their financial futures, but the fundamental reason why the consensus has been so wrong over the credit crunch and the 'recovery' is that few understand the concept of the system limit. From this lack of understanding, flows the erroneous belief that economic relationships work in a set way. From this, incorrect conclusions that inflation is a threat, and that interest rates will rise, themselves follow.

There are likely to be increasingly desperate attempts to create inflation over the next few years. There is a simple reason why these attempts will ultimately fail. When interest rates go down or bank failures threaten, depositors withdraw their money from banks. The bank credit multiplier then goes into reverse, with banks limiting their lending artificially[104]. As a result economic activity slows down further. Only contrarian thinking can provide an alternative. Inability to think differently will lock many investors into declining capital bases and declining income as the financial crisis rolls on.

We live in a pseudo-dictatorship. In Britain, we elect new political dictators every five years then let them get on with it. Politicians, though, are not the real dictators. The real dictators are the consensus opinion-formers. They brook no dissent. Take, as an example, the release of UK GDP figures for the second quarter of 2010. Most newspapers and magazines produced a U-shaped graph showing how the economy had apparently recovered the lost ground. The graph was taken from the British government's National Statistics press release without thought. The impression formed was completely wrong. Why? Because the graph plotted a rate of change, which unfortunately ignored the absolute loss of output. The facts were:

UK GDP 3rd Quarter 2008   £340,780 million

UK GDP 2nd Quarter 2010   £328,766 million

This was the dictatorship of the consensus, followed faithfully in every story. There had been insufficient growth to recover the lost ground, yet nobody recognised this.

Repetition of simplistic, self-evidently "true" stories drove the South Sea bubble, the Japanese bubble, the Technology, Media and Telecommunications bubble, the property bubble and the commodity bubble. It also influenced policy nostrums, such as using higher interest rates to fight inflation, while ignoring the desperate need of the authorities to create inflation and their utter inability to do so. Repetition spread the idea that the dollar needed to be devalued to solve America's financial problems; instead, the dollar rose. This example demonstrates another truth: when found out, the consensus simply move on and ignore their gross error. When the Establishment get it totally wrong, they just forget. Opinion is a fashion business, not a science.

Some examples of group think

Most investors are obsessed with inflation, property and commodities. The obsession was fed by news stories repeating the same "look how well you do" line. It's a form of propaganda, perhaps unintentional, but certainly effective. One absurd news item caught my eye: a report about how investors were buying mobile phone masts to rent out, on the grounds that the yield would be higher than on residential buy-to-let. But the mobile phone business has already peaked and internet based technologies such as voice over internet protocol have started to affect total demand. This is one reason why the mobile industry is in some difficulty, added to overpaying for 3G licences. Mobile phone masts can too easily be made redundant by changes in network topography or demand[105].

As another example, the plan (arising from the European Union) to replace standard light bulbs by low energy models to save energy wasted as heat is an example of group think. Much criticism has been directed to the mercury content of such bulbs, while missing the accounting trick: little or no energy will be saved! Domestic lights are usually on after dark in winter. Summer usage is trivial in comparison. Most homes have central heating. Taking away the heat source of the humble light bulb will lead to the central heating boiler cutting in more often and using *more* energy to maintain the *same* temperature. It is true that there will be a small saving by reducing marginal use of electricity and therefore marginal production of electricity, since fuel conversion to electricity is more expensive than direct use of the same fuel in central heating.

This dominance of group think is not new. It is the converse of Shaw's dictum: 'Reasonable people adapt themselves to the world. Unreasonable people attempt to adapt the world to themselves. All progress, therefore, depends on unreasonable people'.

Those who exploit fashion use the desire of reasonable people to conform with the majority. Fashionable opinions inspire and reinforce group think. Group think is endemic in the way our society is structured. It is not going to vanish. But it extends beyond the media and the way we are conditioned to think.

The world of standards and rules

The system limit threatens finance, but finance cannot be separated from the condition of our society. I describe contemporary society as 'disconnected' because it operates in silos, governed by regulation and compliance.

Let's consider the broad issue of the way western society is managed, which has been hinted at by Gillian Tett in her book *Fool's Gold*. It is common throughout the western world for governments to outsource large sections of their responsibility to delegated bodies. Again, Britain may have led the way in creating delegated bodies that have little or no democratic control.

Delegated bodies are given terms of reference and powers by legislation, sometimes through secondary legislation that receives little or no scrutiny, and may even acquire power to create tertiary legislation. As a result, they are governed in the interests of complying with their statutory objectives. As time moves on, those statutory objectives may lose relevance compared to the pressing national need. As an example, the Financial Services Authority lacks power to consider competition, which itself reduces the chance of market solutions evolving[106]. Statutory objectives and terms of reference always encompass the perceived 'right way' of doing things at the time they are set and thereby become pro-cyclical.

However, delegated bodies are very good at four things. As noted earlier, one is making plenty of rules, which just happen to ossify society and prevent evolution. Sometimes, these rules merely implement higher-level rules made elsewhere, for example in Europe. The second is that they can slowly lose touch with reality, since an unwritten objective of their creation is to protect ministerial reputation. The third is that they spend generously: according to Professor Matthew Flinders[107] Britain may have 5,000 such bodies spending £200 billion per annum, and some may even have lost contact with their sponsoring departments. The fourth is that they enforce static comparisons – are the standards met? – in a world of dynamic change. Judgment that a business cycle exists is replaced by denial that conditions may change[108].

The private sector has also followed the fashion of creating bodies that set standards, write rules, prescribe actions in place of judgment, or simply encourage group think. This is how accountants allowed Enron to grow, then allowed offshore funding entities to contribute to the credit bubble. This is how actuaries allowed pension funds to assume equity out-performance, denying the existence of a long capital market cycle and permitting pension contribution holidays based on the demands of the tax system and optimistic assumptions about values[22].

Once, politics were representative of the people, attracting a broad cross-section of society. More recently, British politics has consisted of a centralised legislative machine pumping out ever broader rule making powers to delegated bodies. The legislative

116

machine has little democratic input; life is governed by rules made by these bodies, leaving the citizen feeling powerless and isolated. These rules can be influenced, but the only effective influence is usually through industry lobby groups operating at the European level. In parallel with the growth of European legislation, lobbying groups have grown in power and influence.

The result is a silo society that loses touch with its common interest. The primary roles of MPs seem to me to be a combination of glorified ombudsmen in their constituencies, tools for the government of the day to impose its wishes through excessively prescriptive legislation and to fight the next election. Cutting MPs off from outside interests can only entrench the silo society[109].

The education system is itself a victim of short-sighted fashions. At one time, intellectual attainment at an early age was fashionable. We threw that away, substituting social engineering. Now that too has given way to a dumbing down process of meaningless targets, as we deny most young people the ability to think, question, or write the Queen's English.

Once upon a time professional skill meant judgment, care and attention, backed up by experience, seeded by training in fundamentals. The whole added up to diversity plus common sense. What is a profession today? It seems little more than ticking the right boxes based on a bureaucratic set of hoops designed to ensure a bland uniformity, supported by endless risk protection – protecting governing bodies and regulators. Ideas contradicting the received wisdom are unwanted. Common sense is frowned upon. Original thought, diversity and evolution have been replaced by procedures, prescription and conformity.

The regulated, compliant society

Britain is now a fairly extreme case of a highly regulated, compliant society. There are so many rules that it is impossible to keep abreast of them all. This explains why officialdom itself falls over occasionally: as I was writing this, I read a report about prosecuting errors made by HM Revenue and Customs. I suspect that the highly regulated nature of British life today is doing economic damage.

British governments have similar and complementary propensities to delegated bodies. They certainly write endless legislation – now often as home-grown additions to European rules. Although British quangos are to be culled, only a little has been done about the burden of excessively detailed legislation. Overheads will only start to fall when the imposed legislative burden is removed. Sadly, there have been many demands for more regulation. If bailouts are doomed to fail by making the total debt burden worse, then more financial regulation will be equally ineffective. The opposite is more likely to be true: take away the cost and safety net of regulation and people will learn to be more prudent. One case of burnt fingers may be sufficient for any individual investor to learn the lesson. The illusion that regulation can fix everything is a dangerous fallacy. Exposing the fallacy will bring two great benefits:

1. Investors will learn prudent behaviour and expect it of their investment managers.

2. When the regulatory straitjacket is curtailed, evolution can be given a chance.

Another damaging British trait has been to encourage unnecessary centralisation. Europe sucked power out of Whitehall, so Whitehall filled the void by sucking power out of local communities. Planning rules, regulations, compliance demands, all strengthen large businesses at the expense of small ones. Thus, small shops are replaced by supermarkets bringing uniformity and scale at the expense of convenience and traffic. Government creates the conditions in which only the large can survive, then tries to assuage concerns with yet more regulation. What happened to competition, enterprise and variety?

'More transparency' is a variant of more regulation. People will be confused by even more detail. If this book achieves anything, it will be to enable an informed general understanding of issues that have been buried in technical detail. Nobody understood the global Ponzi schemes or the precise meaning of accounting standards because there was already far too much detail. 'More transparency' is a cover story for hiding the truth by burying useful nuggets of information in a massive sandcastle.

In addition, the British government has created ever greater overhead costs through the compliance culture. But regulation and compliance are not free goods; their cost is passed back to consumers through higher prices. The problem is no longer the traditional one of 'too much red tape', it is the entire way of life of the regulated society.

Britain's coalition government has fallen for the illusion that more financial regulation must be a good thing. But regulation inhibits evolution. Creating a tough consumer finance regulator will entrench the notions that somebody else should always pay, there should be no risk in depositing money in a bank and investments should always deliver golden returns. The truth is that nanny does not know best[110].

Forty-five years ago, Douglas McGregor described two alternative ways of handling people at work[111]. Theory X said that people had to be controlled and coerced to work; Theory Y that work was as natural as rest or play and people should be allowed to find their own way of working. For the following thirty years, Theory Y was in the ascendant as business prospered. But now Britain is back to Theory X, courtesy of ever more prescriptive legislation. Regulators demand that businesses are run in the style of control freaks, following due process, keeping endless records and complying with equally endless demands: initiative and flexibility are unwanted, in the cause of risk aversion and political correctness.

Regulation causes costs that have largely to be met by the private sector. These costs count, wrongly, as economic growth. Until the credit crunch came along, businesses put their prices up to cover such imposed costs. Now price rises meet customer resistance. The new economic cycle is one of expanding regulatory costs destroying the economy. The Treasury does not even recognise that such a cycle exists. But the cycle will turn, and regulatory make-work will decline as recession deepens. Then regulatory cutbacks will simply reinforce the downward side of the economic cycle.

Conformity

Conformity is particularly inherent in the nature of bureaucratic organisations. You don't get promoted by rocking the boat, insisting that the favoured programme has unrecognised downsides, or observing that chasing the target damages alternative viewpoints. So it is natural that as bureaucratic institutions have strengthened their grip on national life, group think has become more entrenched.

The public sector now imposes received wisdom without recognising its limitations. In summer 2009, one of the journals that circulate in Britain's public sector carried an article by Prof. John Seddon of Cardiff University criticising the mechanistic demands of the Audit Commission[112], showing how their imposed world view damaged the service provided by local government[113]. In financial services, the regulator proposes to encourage standards of advice for the general public that ask practitioners to invest, among other things, in tracker funds. This seemingly innocuous proposal has a hidden downside. It takes two to make a market: price discovery needs differing views. Tracker funds need somebody to trade, make a market and set prices. Already pension funds make extensive use of index tracking. How will the market set prices if even more investors passively follow the trend? Expecting more use of index trackers can only be a pro-cyclical force, adding to market instability as computer driven trades rush hither and thither.[114].

Accountants have also managed to build a precise set of rules to replace judgment and common sense. Once, accountants considered the broad dynamics of a business, how it might

121

change, and the impact of different assumptions, to form a view about the merit of accounts. Nowadays, they simply select which standards to apply and then tick boxes to check compliance with those standards. Regulators demand that standards are followed uncritically: the US Securities and Exchange Commission and the Financial Services Authority both require accounts to comply with standards[115]. Taking banks as an example, auditors can no longer make a judgment that bad debts may rise and therefore extra provisions should be made: the standards prevent individuality or thought[116].

In the days when the early Italian bankers invented debit and credit, there was no European commission or Federal government to lay down detailed prescriptive rules. Nowadays, politicians announce their demands, then set retinues of bureaucrats to work at implementing their grandiose projects. In Europe, the bureaucrats write detailed proposals, 'consult' on how the detail will work to ensure a degree of practicality, then write directives and statutory instruments to implement their design.

The entire structure of standards, rules, regulations and delegated bodies making rules, acts to prevent evolution and reinforce conformity. As bureaucratic institutions have grown in importance, so conformity has entrenched group think. This is the nature of our society. All the cogs follow their rules, but the whole can be a complete nonsense. Only through diversity can there be any hope of spotting what is coming or adapting to change, but diversity is unwanted. Group think will flourish until the power of standards setters and bureaucracies is curtailed. Since the reaction to the credit crunch has been to propose more rules and tighter standards, it is a fair bet that more financial crises will follow.

One of the remarkable points that I have found in writing this book is that many of the detailed errors, incorrect policies et al, have already been amply documented by others. But we never learn. The delegated society, the strength of lobby groups and vulnerability of our political system to pressure, the sheer volume of noise in the media and on the Internet, the immediacy of the demands of daily life, all combine to make our collective memory rather short.

7 Academic differences of opinion

In 2009, *The Economist* tried to analyse how academic communities had missed what was going on[117]. It made a case for finance and economics professionals to get together and understand one another better, so as to avoid errors such as these:

◆ caveats being ignored;

◆ silly assumptions being made (e.g., house prices always rise);

◆ models assuming that capital markets work perfectly.

We have already seen how politicians, accountants and actuaries lost the broad picture in the years preceding the credit crunch. Now let's look at the contribution of economists and financial academics.

The differing economic arguments

In his book *The Trouble with Markets*, Roger Bootle lists failings in two particular professions – financial advisers[118] and economists (his own profession)[119]. The economics profession has started a debate about why it failed to see anything coming at all. It seems to me that there are four groups out there, arguing different cases. They are:

• the Keynesians, who advocate financial stimulus by creating more debt;

• the Ricardians, who argue for policies of debt

repayment;

- those who believe economic activity can be predicted from behaviour;

- those who admit theories are inadequate.

Until May 2010, British politicians were offering endless jam today, paid for by mortgaging the future, in the charming belief that such policies were Keynesian and therefore must be 'a good thing'. To say the Keynesians were in control is itself a simplification. In the great credit boom of the 1990s and again following the dot-com bust, politicians preferred to encourage the expansion, which is why the subsequent bust was so severe[120]. The Keynesians are still in control in America and France.

The Keynesian camp believe more government spending will create growth through the multiplier effect which will allow the deficits to be repaid from future economic recovery. Their argument depends on banks willingly lending extra credit created by governments, and businesses and families eagerly borrowing this credit. They argue that a little more debt should create much more economic activity, enabling the original debt to be repaid once recession ends. But it's obvious that the linkage has failed, because banks are reporting less lending and even if the linkage did hold, why should more debt be self-repaying? It was true in the great inflation when interest rates were below the rate of inflation, but the last quarter century has seen stubbornly positive real interest rates, that is the cost of borrowing staying above the rate of inflation – so even if the extra debt got out there, it would not achieve its objective.

Keynesian policies are yesterday's answer to a different world which had not reached the system limit. Governments have already purloined the earning capacity of the next two generations at least, in order to pay for the world's existing borrowing. In the short run, Keynesian policies buy time, as banks stay afloat, financial speculation revives and share and commodity prices bubble away. It seems to me that the cost will be a worse problem later as the cost of servicing extra debt starts to bite.

Those economists who don't accept the Keynesian consensus, generally follow Ricardian principles, which are that extra spending produces neither extra economic activity nor extra tax revenue and is therefore self-defeating. The Ricardians reckon that rising deficits are unsustainable. The cost of servicing the debt being created will exceed any benefit achieved, bringing no overall improvement. The policy prescription adopted by the Ricardians is the exact opposite of that recommended by the Keynesians. The rush to austerity is an extreme case of Ricardian principle.

The third group are the behaviourists. They say that if we can predict how people react to policy changes, then we can work out precisely what to do. This is the predict and control illusion that has led (for example) to the regulatory nonsenses of elaborate bank capital structures and requirements, recalculated daily, but completely missing the real risks.

The tiny, fourth, group consists of a handful of economists who can see that none of the theories work and have begun to consider alternatives. One correspondent writing to the *Financial Times* proposed that economics should be declared a failing discipline, economists as not fit for purpose, and a physicist put in charge of sorting their theories out. I hope the concept of the system limit will interest those economists who accept the sterility of the stimulus vs. austerity argument. Certainly, those not privy to such academic debates, remain suspicious that the elaborate models used by economists may be built on dubious foundations[121].

Is financial theory bunk?

Contemporary financial theory has been built on two principles, the Capital Asset Pricing Model and Black-Scholes-Merton pricing of derivatives. Regulators have added a third, Value at Risk. Let's briefly review them.

The Capital Asset Pricing Model attempts to value a security by comparing its riskiness to the risk-free rate of return. I believe there is a fundamental error here: it is the concept that there is such a thing as a risk-free rate of return. Of course, it is possible to have a relative comparison for the risk-free return, for example to a Treasury Bill. But such relativities are only valid over short time periods, since the comparison base itself changes. There have been recent occasions when the yield on Treasury Bills has been zero, giving no risk-free return.

In order to understand the limitation of this, we need to imagine a new company that starts as a family business, then issues shares to raise capital. Let's suppose that the shares are issued at £1. The company becomes fashionable and many more investors buy in the secondary market (which is what stock markets are), pushing the price up to £10. They purchase shares from the original family investors. Then the buyers disappear, the company does not do as well as hoped, and sellers predominate. As a result, the share price starts to fall. The original investors buy back their shares from the later ones to reassert control.

What will happen to the share price?

I posed this question once in a public lecture that I gave, and the replies were interesting. Most participants thought that the share price would simply go back to £1, since the original investors would be left holding their original shares. The few who differed thought the price should settle at a higher level.

What would happen, though, is that the share price would be *lower* than £1. The reason is that all the frictional costs of running markets – price spreads, trading costs, regulations – would be reflected in the price. Going back to square one reveals the hidden costs. Far from having a risk-free return, there is a time period loss involved.

Once you question the notion of a risk-free return, then the Capital Asset Pricing Model becomes somewhat less attractive. There are other faults as well: the Capital Asset Pricing Model is itself built on another theory, that markets are efficient (the Efficient Markets Hypothesis). This ignores the endless speculative rises and crashes that tell us that markets are anything but efficient.

Black-Scholes-Merton is a mathematical model for predicting option (i.e. derivative) prices, based on the price of the underlying security and assuming a risk-free return. It is open to the objection that mass delusions (crowd and group behaviour) do not conform to such assumptions. Financial market practitioners are just as susceptible to such mass delusions as the general public. The limitations of this theory have been amply covered in *Lecturing Birds on Flying*, in which Pablo Triana says that the theory isn't used in practice, does not work and was not original. These limitations may explain some of the catastrophes in capital markets in recent years. Certainly, the key assumption that investment returns follow a normal probability distribution[122] has been found wanting in every crash.

'Value at Risk' requires a bank to calculate capital reserves by applying a precise percentage to each liability it has, the percentage charge varying by the type of liability. In theory, riskier liabilities should carry a higher capital charge. The normal probability distribution that so failed to foresee the unexpected losses made is an underlying assumption of 'Value at Risk', yet 'Value at Risk' is still the basis by which regulators set bank capital requirements.

This gives us a clue to one of the problems of the disconnected society. Regulators use 'Value at Risk' because academics promote it. Governments, regulators and quangos usually call on experts to tell them what to do. If the theory that experts produce has limitations, those taking expert advice are hardly likely to understand the limitations. How many financial market officials foresaw that the normal probability distribution would fail and therefore understood the limitations of the policies they were adopting before the event? The whole set-up of delegated bodies employing experts is in danger of entrenching received wisdom uncritically.

When you consider how frequently the models fail, perhaps because of their reliance on the normal probability distribution, the inevitable conclusion has to be that much financial modelling is of limited use. The same goes for economic modelling, which simply failed to understand that people's behaviour would change and therefore the relationships would change[123]. When will the academia of both finance and economics admit that the real issues are crowd delusions and conformity rather than the assumptions of their present models?

8 The dark side of capital markets

Investment advice is a fashion business. During the sixty years following 1945, governments set out to deliberately manage economies using the credit expansion tool. The great inflation followed, then the great move to equity investment. Since the system limit now prevents the tool from working, capital market behaviour must be affected.

Japan gives us a clue as to the nature of the change. For twenty years, Japanese bond yields have trended downwards to unheard of low levels as bond prices have risen[124]. For the same twenty years, Japanese equity prices have declined, rallied and then declined even further. Japanese stock markets have been an effective mechanism for destroying savings. Every proclamation that the Japanese bear market was over has fallen by the wayside, leaving the experts without credibility. The inability to foresee how Japan's capital markets would behave follows directly from the system limit and the policy contradictions that Japan experienced more than a decade before the West.

The capital market cycle

Capital markets follow a long cycle, beyond the experience of most practitioners, detectable only by understanding history and then applying this understanding to contemporary conditions. The principles are identical for any market where prices depend on the supply of credit: equities, bonds, property and commodities are all markets where prices must relate to the availability of credit. Bond prices prosper when credit is lacking, while the other three prosper when credit is abundant.

The whole market cycle consists of bull market followed by bear market, as surely as night follows day. The bull market in assets is driven by an increasing supply of credit and economic expansion, since more credit leads to higher prices. The bear market in assets is driven by less credit and economic contraction; there is no purchasing power to keep asset prices high. Only fixed interest bonds are contra-cyclical, declining in price as credit expands and rising in price as credit shrinks[125].

There are two useful theories for analysing the whole market cycle: conversion flow and Dow theory.

Conversion flow

Long-term trends progress over time periods of decades. Gradually, pundits, advisers and the investing public notice that there is a trend in place. In a bull market, rising prices bring out the buyers, since people are comfortable with past performance and trend following. The rising market, whatever it is in, becomes fashionable. As prices rise, belief starts to form and most are converted to believing in the trend. By the time the market peaks, there is nobody left to convert: there is complete unison about the merits of the class of investment. This is the process of conversion flow.

Thereafter, conversion flow goes into reverse. Prices fall a little and although most believe the bull market is intact, a few realise a peak has been reached and take their money away. Conversion flow then continues until the fashion has been entirely forgotten.

At the bottom of the bear market cycle, nobody is left believing in the merits of the former fashion.

Returning to our example of Japan, conversion flow has been running away from Japanese equities for twenty years. But there is another condition for a market bottom. It is the inverse of the extensive speculation that accompanies every market peak: total disbelief. The unison that proclaimed a market peak becomes the chorus that says "Never!" Since investment advisers are still arguing the case for investing in Japanese equities, I conclude that the great Japanese equity bear market is nowhere near over.

Another lesson can be gleaned from Japan. Share price rallies lasted two or three years. They allowed pundits to claim the end of the bear market, only to be wrong footed by the new declines that followed. Much the same has happened in Britain and America as the dot-com bust gave way to a false boom and then the credit crunch.

The greater fool theory

The greater fool theory is another aspect of conversion flow. The theory is that when you buy an investment, you should expect to sell it at a profit. Therefore the person you sell to must also expect to sell at a profit. Since no investment goes up for ever, the later buyer is taking a little more risk than the earlier buyer. The earliest buyer of all, of course, is the wise one who is prepared to go against the crowd of fashion when sentiment is at an extreme negative, then wait patiently for years until the tide turns his or her way.

The point about the greater fool theory is that eventually the greatest fool of all appears. The greatest fools are buyers with nobody to sell to: those who cannot understand why they get it wrong. Markets have been full of people who just had to buy property for their pension. As both prices and rents fall, their pension funds are likely to be somewhat disappointed. What an investor should aim for is to have the cash to buy when the market has only sellers and no buyers. For property markets, a longer period of time may be needed to reach this point than for stock markets, since property responds slowly to changes in conditions.

The story that 'Japan is different', widely touted in 1989 and 1990, typified a peak in the cycle of foolishness. Those greater fools were stalking the City and Wall Street again in 1999 and yet again in 2006 and early 2007, just as they were stalking Tokyo in 1989.

Both conversion flow and the greater fool theory show the importance of fashion – and of getting off the fashion bandwagon in good time, before the market turns, rather than waiting for difficult selling conditions.

Dow theory of 'bear' markets

Dow theory is over a century old, largely forgotten, yet still relevant. The principle is that each and every bear market consists of three downward drives in prices, linked by major rallies.

1. The first downward drive is the 'bolt from the blue' that nobody sees coming, the subsequent rally giving credibility to claims that it was an aberration and the bull market remains intact. But the rally rarely retraces

the lost ground and a new downward drive in prices
follows.

2. This new decline takes prices down to a much lower
    level. Unlike the bolt from the blue, this period is
    driven by investors selling in response to falling prices
    and generally deteriorating economic and business
    news. Following the price falls, a new counter-trend
    rally emerges bringing a period of calm.

3. Then the third downward price drive arrives. Investors
    dump their investments in despair, fearing that any
    company may go bust leaving worthless shares.
    Dumping occurs at price levels less than a quarter of
    those at the previous peak (in 1932, the bottom of the
    Dow Jones index was at an 89% loss). Panic selling
    marks a market bottom just as speculation marks a
    market top.

Within those five stages, three downward and two upward, there
can be many shorter-term price trends. It is my view that the first
of Dow's three stages occurred between April 2000 and March
2003 and a four-year counter-trend rally followed. The credit
crunch started the second stage, with the post-Lehman rally
forming an intermediate counter-trend within an ongoing bear
market.

Practical perspectives

Dow theory gives us a conceptual framework for estimating the
overall progress of a cyclical bear market. It has no relation to
arbitrary price change definitions used by many investment

advisers, though it does help recognise counter-trend rallies as part of an ongoing bear market rather than erroneously describing them as new bull markets.

I refuse to categorise a bear market as one in which prices have fallen by any particular percentage. This great bear market started in April 2000 in the West and after one decade it is nowhere near over. I noted the policy lessons from Japan in chapter 4: all policy options fail because there is too much debt. The market lesson from Japan is equally uncomfortable: once the equity cult ends, it does not return.

At a market top, shares change hands on price to earnings ratios of 20 or more and dividend yields of 1% or 2%. At the bottom, those dividend yields will reach double figures even though cash dividends will be much lower as companies seek to conserve their resources; price to earnings ratios will be in low single figures. Such comparisons can be established from market conditions in New York in 1932 and London in 1974. The great Japanese bear market is nowhere near a climax of despair after two decades. Why should the West be any different?

Time

In bear markets, many investors hold on hoping to recover their lost ground, only to sell later at lower prices. Average performance statistics are used to justify losses. Only by thinking in very long time-frames, taking account of the long capital market cycle, can the investor hope to achieve better than average performance. Such a philosophy is in complete contradiction to the urge to do something, which the investment management industry constantly promotes. It is the antithesis of active investment.

There is an extreme form of active investment, which has emerged in the last three years: high frequency trading. It is likely, though impossible to prove conclusively, that it accounts for the more extreme market movements of recent years. Specialist traders, hedge funds and investment banks position computers in stock exchange premises so as to gain advantages in milliseconds and use complex algorithms to generate many purchases and sales every second; some of their trades are orders that are cancelled before execution. It is estimated that half of trades in the London stock market and some 60% in New York are computer generated in this way. There have been suggestions that the 'flash crash' of 6th May 2010 may have been caused, at least in part, by high frequency trading amplifying a genuine sale and there have also been suggestions that cancelling orders milliseconds after placing them may be affecting pricing.

My concern is much broader. In the 1987 crash, now ancient history to probably 90% of market participants, just twelve institutions were actively selling in New York using computer program trades. It is obvious that the majority in 1987 were, in effect, following short-term trends. Are contemporary sharp rises and falls in a day the result of similar copycat behaviour? Trend following is greatly in vogue as an investment style. At its simplest, it consists of replicating an index. In a wider sense, it is the driving force behind market rallies and declines[126]. How many of these computer algorithms that dominate markets are mimicking each other? How many are contrarian, buying when others are selling and selling when others are buying? It should be obvious that if the two groups are unequal then high frequency trading must destabilise markets and have, at least, the potential to cause mayhem.

How did serious investment, which requires analysis, thought, and an element of judgment, come to be replaced by such rapid automated responses to market movements? In this way, high frequency traders, program traders, day traders and index investors ensure they become part of the crowd moving the market. Such mass behaviour is a symptom of the system limit, a treadmill that can have few winners.

Propaganda

Investment advice treads the boards of the catwalk, with fashions emerging then fading away. Who now remembers Japanese warrants, all the rage some twenty-five years ago? Why do the public now obsess about inflation, when the government bond market – the best discounting mechanism there is – is signalling loud and clear that deflation lies ahead? Why have investors run after property when it is grossly overpriced?

The propaganda war follows conversion flow. At a market top, there are only speculators and no doubters. We have lived through the comment and opinion accompanying such a period. Now new stories must come to the surface. Here are some examples:

1. Equities are cheap now. *In a bear market, they continue to get cheaper.*

2. It's too late to sell now. *That is what the pundits said when Japan was down only 25%.*

3. People have to eat: buy food shares. *The price at which shares changed hands fell by 75% to 90% in past bear markets, even for businesses that stayed around. Those businesses that went bust, for whatever reason, left worthless share certificates. Companies go bust for many reasons, for example too much debt or a management mistake, which can happen in any business.*

4. This is a bond bubble. *To be a bubble, there must be unanimity that you should only invest in bonds and nothing else. There is no such unanimity of comment. Even Japan, with its ten year lead over the West, does not provoke opinions that investors should only buy bonds.*

Conditions for the 'bear' market to end

Going against prevailing sentiment, lying low for years, is never popular. Yet sentiment can be used to recognise some major turning points. The panic to buy anything with the flavour of 'new economy' in the great internet bubble was one example. Another was the mad rush into property between 2003 and 2007. Both of these were examples of the rule that the most intense speculation occurs at a market top, since few will speculate on something that is down and out[127]. Senseless speculation always marks a market peak, and the reports of 'open house' viewing and sales in London at Easter 2007 were a perfect sell signal. For an example of the opposite extreme, consider the sentiment expressed about conventional Gilts in 1990, when the *Financial Times* wrote a headline "Gilts – do you really need them[128]?" As a contrarian, that headline led me to recommend my clients selling all index linked stock and buying conventional fixed coupon Gilts. At the time, few could see that inflation would tumble down from the 10% level, or interest rates from the 15% level. Even fewer could see the attraction of locking into Gilt yields of 12% to 13% for up to thirty years.

So a long-term, patient investor, will buy when others are selling, sell when others are buying and keep a low profile for years in between. Contrarians never appeal to the majority and invariably look wrong at turning points. Thus, pundits can have a field day: just look at the way the late Mr Tony Dye of Phillips and Drew (now part of UBS) was pilloried for his 'error' of saying stock markets were too high and daring to keep 15% in cash. But then, such opinions are a rarity.

Shares will be cheap when there are only sellers and no buyers; when prices are a tenth or less of their previous peak, across the board; when both share prices and cash dividends have dropped but share prices have dropped faster producing the bizarre statistic of double figure dividend yields on lower cash returns; when every newspaper reports horror stories of how readers have been wiped out in capital markets; when regulators cancel their proposed rules requiring investment advisers to recommend tracker funds and unit trusts and replace them by rules requiring investment advisers to recommend government bonds; when you hear at the golf club of members who have told their brokers to sell everything. These are typical of the conditions I shall be looking for in order to buy.

By the end of this bear market, we must expect some well-known companies to have disappeared for ever, not just the handful of banks that have vanished so far. The life cycle of companies is remarkably short. I have the 1960 edition of *Beginners Please*, the standard Investors Chronicle handbook, in my library. Many of the 30 shares in the FT index then (there was no 100 share index) have gone bust, restructured (with shareholder losses), or been taken over, disappearing without trace. Just one out of thirty retains its original name and remains within the modern FTSE 100 index[129]. The 1973-75 bear market saw a few off; many more disappeared as Britain's manufacturing sector was decimated. This great bear market will also claim its victims.

What should investors do in this great 'bear' market?

Investors have expected ludicrous returns and financial market players apparently found ways to satisfy them. Many products were designed to be saleable in retail markets, using assumptions about future share price rises creating vehicles to produce high income at the expense of capital. The underlying assumptions were often somewhat optimistic; the mechanism usually involved complex derivatives. But the highly geared players are now steadily being found out. Counter-party risk has been discovered following the demise of Lehman Brothers; the number of failing hedge funds is rising; the incestuous and circuitous nature of derivatives is being exposed. Declining availability of bank credit is hitting private equity buyouts.

Failed financial schemes rarely come to light in the good times. They burst into the open when markets turn down. Given the extent of financial alchemy now unwinding, the extent of the declines still to come cannot be minor. The only issue seems to be whether the 89% loss of 1929 to 1932[130] will prove a barrier. It will be some years before the answer is known.

The existence of so many bloated asset classes in recent years, driven up purely by new investor demand fuelled by expansionary credit, should give concern. There is ample evidence that property markets are bloated. In *Fantasy Island*, Atkinson and Elliott described Britain's economy as being sodden with debt, built on property speculation. The two are opposite sides of the same coin: the coin is common currency throughout the world. It is the growth of credit that has led to the inflation fear and the growth of its twin, debt, that is throttling economies slowly.

I have argued for years that there is acute financial risk. This less pleasant aspect of capitalism is one of the facts of investment life. The only viable strategy throughout this long-drawn-out crash will be to have your own directly invested portfolio of government bonds. Eventually, all other investment options will simply wither on the vine as share prices continue their long bear market, property prices trend slowly downwards and bad debts rise everywhere. The weaker governments may be downgraded by the ratings agencies and some may even partially default on their debt. However, in a system with no precious metal standard, government bonds of the largest nations will be the *relative* winners.

There is a fundamental difference between government bonds and corporate bonds. It is the strength of the guarantor, government or merely a company. If a company's profits fall so much that interest cannot be paid, its bond prices fall. The historic yield then looks attractive. The attraction is superficial; risk is real. In extremis, the company ceases to exist and its debt is worthless. Corporate bonds can sometimes involve as much risk as share prices.

Share prices have already fallen in recognition of future risk. The fall in price comes first, then the dividend cut comes several years later. This is why buying apparently high dividend yields with good dividend cover does not work in a broad downturn: cash payouts to shareholders fall as companies seek to conserve their cash[131]. Stock market indices can be particularly misleading, since they are regularly revised to eliminate falling shares and substitute rising ones. Those portfolios which retain the falling shares therefore slip behind the index: the index takes on a life of its own.

Capital markets now involve serious risks. For individuals, there is no equity, property or commodity based strategy that will consistently exploit an unpredictable series of financial dislocations. Since these investments are no longer viable, the only rule is to **stand aside and let others make the mistakes**[132].

9 The attitude change

The opposite policies of stimulus and austerity both bring undesirable consequences.

Additional stimulus creates further unaffordable debt. Yet if the policy were to be successful, extra debt would lead to even more defaults. A rise in defaults would then threaten the solvency of lending institutions.

The austerity alternative shrinks economies. With less work, citizens will find it harder to service and repay existing debts, possibly creating a new wave of defaults, which in turn will also threaten lenders' solvency.

So long as thinking is constrained to these two alternatives, economies will deteriorate and times get tougher. Far from the growth paraded by the perennial optimists, the public will find household finances slowly ground down by lack of work, higher taxes and the cost of servicing household debt, encouraging misery and social unrest. The downward trend in house prices will destroy savings as gearing (leverage) works in reverse. The costs of meeting pension fund obligations will either hurt companies, pensioners or both. It is no longer possible to borrow imaginary money from the future.

The bubble economy has given the West both the consumer society and the compensation culture. It has enabled generations of politicians to pull mythical policy levers to bring apparent prosperity for all. The long slow grind that people now face is the price to pay for all past credit expansion.

In Britain, if successful, Quantitative Easing combined with public sector austerity will transfer public sector debt to the private sector. But the private sector does not wish to borrow more and will frustrate Quantitative Easing. In America, Quantitative Easing combined with more economic stimulus is an attempt to inflate existing debt away by creating more: absurd. By expressing these policies in such stark terms, it becomes evident how futile they are. The futility is driven by the Establishment's belief that debt can expand indefinitely[133].

Regulation failed to foresee the deep change in the financial system, so why should more regulation work? The official policy of "lend more, regulate more" is thwarted by the practicalities of the system limit. But there are other reasons why regulation is not the answer. We have already discussed the silo society, with its inability to take the broad view. I hope also to have shown how history is relevant to understanding markets. Now I want to introduce an archaeological perspective.

In his book *The Collapse of Complex Societies*[134], Joseph Tainter showed how the sudden end of the Mayan and other civilisations could be explained by the declining marginal return on investment in complexity. Sophisticated societies continually add to their complexity, since early growth phases bring greatly increased benefits from more complexity. But complexity becomes a machine with a life of its own, and once the marginal return falls below its cost, then the society is steadily undermined. Thus the theoretical aligns with the practical: more regulation is self-destructive.

There is now a deep challenge. The debt-based system cannot exceed the system limit. The challenge is to allow the debt-based system to wither slowly, without precipitating a solvency crisis in our banks and thereby destroying Western society as we know it. Evolution is needed: original ideas that nobody has thought of, to bring forward alternatives to debit and credit. After all, the invention of debit and credit was original at the time: there were no rules to prevent such new ideas emerging from the early Italian bankers.

Islamic banking offers a clue to the possibilities of evolution. It consists of shared ventures, shared ownership of businesses and shared risks. Evolution could well bring forth other alternatives, but our present mindset is actively preventing it. With less regulation, a system lacking debt-based lending may have a chance to emerge. New ideas need to be encouraged rather than squashed. There are already examples of new ideas for shared property and shared ownership in specific areas, brought forth by Internet entrepreneurs: as examples, shared cars, shared parking, micro-investment. Any of these could be another path to a financial system without debt.

There has also been a proposal for a massive debt to equity conversion[135]. If such a solution is viable then it will also emerge through evolution, rather than being designed by bureaucratic fief.

The nations that will make progress and initiate new ideas will be those that encourage business, make individuals responsible for their own actions, encourage market mechanisms and generally avoid extensive regulation and restriction in the majority of areas, not just in finance. They will be nations with diversity of thought rather than the group think which makes so many conform with the way things are.

This, then, is how to move forward. Restrict financial regulation to bank capital structures only, sweep away the overhead cost and complexity of much other regulation, including non-financial regulation so that the diminishing returns of more complexity are reversed, evolution can flourish, and the risk of a social collapse caused by the weight of regulation can be reduced. In the United Kingdom, restricting the effect of defamation law should encourage freedom of speech and thereby enable market reputation to work effectively. All the professions that have acquired narrow silo mentalities based on following extensive rules need to reconnect with the broad interest of society, replacing these petty rules by professional judgment.

Footnotes

1   *Fantasy Island*, Larry Elliott and Dan Atkinson, Constable & Robinson 2007.

2   *The Black Swan*, Nassim Nicholas Taleb, Allen Lane 2007 (UK), Random House 2007 (USA).

3   *Lecturing Birds on Flying: Can Mathematical Theories Destroy the Financial Markets?* Pablo Triana, © Wiley 2009, reprinted with permission of John Wiley & Sons, Inc.

4   *Verdict on the Crash*, Ed. Philip Booth, The Institute of Economic Affairs 2009.

5   *Fool's Gold*, Gillian Tett, Little, Brown Book Group 2009.

6   The system limit is currently a problem for Western countries and Japan. Less developed countries will reach it in time if they continue with similar policies of credit expansion.

7   *The Debt Threat*, Tim Congdon, Basil Blackwell 1988. Congdon gave evidence that there is a limit to debt growth to the House of Commons Treasury and Civil Service Committee in 1986 and published his work more extensively in his book. More recently, similar points have appeared from American economists Carmen Reinhardt and Ken Rogoff, who have argued that debt levels cannot exceed 90% of GDP.

8   The credit created by Quantitative Easing has to go somewhere, and the link to food and commodity price inflation may be through Exchange Traded Funds. It seems that every attempt to open the credit floodgates is followed within a year or two by rising inflation, but the inflation dies away again when the problems caused by excess credit overwhelm the system. See also "Why exchange traded funds give uneasy sense of déjà vu," Gillian Tett, *Financial Times*, 6th May 2011.

9   *The Economist*, 29th April 2010, *The Eurozone debt crisis*, and also

6th May 2010.

10   During the 1987 stock market crash, the Federal Reserve announced that it would stand behind the financial system. As a result, credit continued to expand for the twenty years from that event until the credit crunch. I use the term 'credit interlude' to describe this period, since I believe it is an aberration.

11   Cattle were probably exchanged before coinage was introduced.

12   See *RSA Journal*, Winter 2009, *Policymaking the Darwinist Way* by David Sloan Wilson. Also see www.evolution-institute.org

13   Irving Fisher's theory of debt deflation following the bursting of a credit bubble, in my view, remains valid. The steps he described were:

   i.   Debt liquidation and distress sales.

   ii.   Loans paid off, leading to less money supply.

   iii. Prices fall.

   iv.   Businesses lose asset value and go bust.

   v.   Profits fall.

   vi.   Less output, less trade, more unemployment.

   vii. General loss of confidence.

   viii. Savers hoard money rather than spend.

   ix.   Nominal interest rates fall, real rates rise. [Note: real rates are nominal rates minus inflation. If inflation is -1% and nominal rates +1%, the real rate is 2%.]

14   *Extraordinary Popular Delusions and the Madness of Crowds*, Charles Mackay, originally published 1841. There are many editions available. This and Le Bon (see note 98 below) are still, in my opinion, the best two finance textbooks.

15   Britain left the gold standard in 1914, returned to it in 1925

and finally left it for good in 1931.

16   The rate was altered in 1933.

17   Prior to the advent of managed economies, prices were stable for over three centuries, and expected to be so.

18   *The Downwave*, Robert Beckman, Milestone Publications 1983.

19   Budget 2005. See also *The Daily Telegraph*, 11th June 2011, Billions Squandered by Labour, Robert Winnett, James Kirkup and Holly Wall.

20   Some services, such as new railways, are really infrastructure taking much longer to plan and develop. They fall outside this theory.

21   Note the difference from Japan's forthcoming rebuilding: the background was an expanding credit supply that people were willing to take up and spend productively, whereas Japan now faces the credit aversion that accompanies deflation.

22   In the United Kingdom, taxation was a factor in reducing company pension scheme contributions.

23   *The Great Stagnation*, Tyler Cowen, Dutton 2011.

24   The reporting of broad money growth in the UK has changed but statistics on the National Statistics website show that seasonally adjusted M4 lending was growing at about 12% per annum just before the credit crunch. UK inflation averaged just under 3% per annum from 1985 to 2005. A table of quarterly real GDP growth (adjusted for inflation) on the Guardian website shows that real GDP growth in the UK was around 0.4% to 1.2% per annum from 1997 to 2001, then fell back slightly. It seems, therefore, that roughly two-thirds of money supply growth was disappearing.

25   America leads the way, with Britain following. See *Financial Times*, 26th March 2011 for a detailed analysis of the forthcoming rise in British repossessions: *Double trouble*, Steven

Bernard, Cynthia O'Murcha and Martin Stabe.

26 A charity dedicated to health service improvement.

27 There are many references available to PFI in hospitals. For a discussion see *British Medical Journal* 2003; 326.7395.905 (Edinburgh Royal Infirmary), 2002; 324.7347.1205 and 2002; 324.7347.1178 (bed counts).

28 Table B.24 in Annex B to the 2006 Pre-Budget report* disclosed total payments of £161.4 bn in respect of PFI deals signed at December 2006 for the next 26 years. This included the failed Tube PFI, but only up to 2018-19 as there was a review clause in the Tube PFI contracts. The Taxpayers' Alliance worked through then Treasury data (*PFI Millstone – How heavy is it now?* www.taxpayersalliance.com, Mike Denham, 9th June 2009) and found that the total cash flows to pay for PFI amounted to £206.6 bn until 2041. Discounted at 4.5% (a rate chosen because it was the cost of financing by selling Gilts at the time), the current liability in 2009 came to £124 bn. The Office for Health Economics made the point that, given the taxpayer is going to pay in the end, there was no macro-economic reason for preferring PFI to Exchequer financing.

* Crown Copyright. Crown copyright material is reproduced with the permission of the Controller of HMSO and the Queen's Printer for Scotland

29 The same applies to secondary debt of small building societies (Dunfermline before it failed), structured products and guaranteed bonds of various kinds (Lehman) and other high-risk debt instruments that will be exposed as the depression rolls on.

30 *Financial Times*, 1st April 2008, *Private equity – a clumsy trick with too much debt*, Paul Murphy.

31 *Financial Times*, 2nd April 2008, *Failure rates soar for buy-out*

companies, Gwen Robinson.

32   US accounts have long required precise obedience to detailed standards. The cult of international harmonisation has restricted the UK practice of allowing audit judgment to override standards in order to produce a 'true and fair view'.

33   The taxation problem arising from capitalising knowledge is political. If the rate of tax was low enough so as not to be a disincentive to business, then taxation would not matter that much.

34   The price of an equity share can be argued to be at least partly marginal, since share prices are subject to extremes of over valuation and under valuation, as recent years have demonstrated. It is debatable whether the value of a business is represented by multiplying the number of shares in issue by the share price.

35   The same observation about depending too much on modelling can be applied to global warming models, that have had some difficulty predicting a decade of falling temperatures.

36   Letter from the Chairman of the Netherlands Authority for the Financial Markets, *Financial Times* 2nd April 2009, *Stop political pressure on accounting standard setters*. The writer argues that those setting accounting standards need more independence, rather than becoming part of the political process.

37   *Financial Times*, 27th April 2009. See also *Financial Times*, 11th May 2010 for a proposal to end this, *Accounts body seeks new rules for banks' debts*, Rachel Sanderson.

38   The evidence from the credit crunch is that contingent liabilities do break out sooner or later. The problem is that accounts only crystallise risk when there is some certainty that

it will happen. At the least, a judgment override is needed, since lack of certainty does not mean risk will go away.

39 Such risks can also be distinguished by using the term "uncertainty" to describe outcomes whose odds cannot be calculated. By definition, probabilistic models cannot capture such risks.

40 The market value of Credit Default swaps alone was estimated at $45 trillion in mid-2007 (Charles R. Morris, *The Trillion Dollar Meltdown*, Public Affairs 2008 *). By summer 2008, it was reported as $62 trillion which is close to world Gross Domestic Product. (*Financial Times*, 8th August 2008, *Get a grip on derivatives*, Anuj Gangahar)

* Copyright © 2008 Charles R. Morris, data reproduced by permission of Public Affairs, a member of the Perseus Books Group

41 Stopping the tax deductibility of debt interest would hit many financial schemes, and would need to be phased in slowly to avoid forced economic contraction. Overall, it would nudge the Western financial system more towards the Islamic model (see discussion in chapter 5).

42 "The assumed benefits of higher returns come as lower costs today." This report of a lecture by Andrew Smithers can be found on www.safehaven.com via Google.

43 *The Wall Street Journal Europe*, 27th March 2008, leading article *Uncle Sam stocks up*. The British government has been encouraging the same argument for Northern Rock's pension fund.

44 There was a flurry of press reports about this in summer 2005. See, for example, *Financial Times*, 2nd August 2005, Lombard column and *Pension rules allow 'smoothed' profits*, Norma Cohen, the following day.

45 Another reason for being suspicious about deficit accounting

is that it is formed from static comparisons based on data that must change as the dynamics change.

46   *Financial Times* 2nd May 2011, *NAO warns on cost of public pensions*, Nicholas Timmins.

47   According to Neil Record, *Sir Humphrey's Legacy*, Institute of Economic Affairs 2006, official estimates for the true liability in respect of public sector pension commitments are significantly understated – another long-term financial problem for Britain.

48   Accounting Standards Board discussion paper PN 320, 31st January 2008. See http://www.frc.org.uk/asb/press/pub1513.html

49   *Financial Times*, 15th July 2008, *Alert on pension scheme liabilities*, Jennifer Hughes.

50   An internet search in March 2008 for "Alternative investment summit 2006" produced several conferences with similar titles around the world. Another bubble?

51   The page can be found on the wayback machine, www.archive.org – search for www.terrapinn.com and select a date in September 2005 then "Finance and investment."

52   Legally, a company cannot refuse to fund its pension deficit. The attitude is more likely to be "What must be done to stop these deficits worsening? For one last time, what changes can we make to ensure there are no more demands for further funding of investment losses?"

53   However, a peer review is now required.

54   Figures taken from the website of actuarial consulting firm Barnett Waddingham http://www.barnett-waddingham.co.uk /news/2005/07/accounting-for-pension-costs-under-frs17-2004-survey/. At the end of 2006, the average assumed equity return was +7.75%; three companies in the survey had reduced their assumed return from the previous year, while

seven had assumed a better return than previously.

55   Pension funds are now reported to be cutting back on equity investment: *Financial Times*, 1st April 2008 (*Pension funds sell more equities*, Norma Cohen). There are two issues that follow. One is, who is buying from them? It seems that private investors may have fallen for the "shares now give a wonderful yield" argument, oblivious to the dividend cuts and further capital losses that are likely to lie ahead. The second is, what are pension funds doing with the money? It may be that they have been buying more alternative investments, another cause of rising commodity prices, damaging to the very present and future pensioners they serve. Or perhaps they have been buying gold, just before the IMF starts a five-year sale programme? It is possible that share prices will fall faster than the cutbacks, in which case deficits will balloon. All these uncertainties reinforce the point that there are no longer any easy answers.

56   Although the levy has now been changed to be lower for over-funded schemes and higher for under-funded schemes, it retains a penalty element for "good" schemes by deliberately capping the charge to weak schemes.

57   New European solvency rules will add to the strain.

58   Of course, many will live in hope that the bear market has ended, or will shortly end. The complex dilemma of collective fund design affects the new state-sponsored UK pension funds. Unable to go against the crowd, needing to balance the interests of different age groups, how can a default investment option be designed? In my view, the problem is insoluble so long as collectivisation and abdication of individual investment responsibility go hand in glove and are viewed with disregard to the long-term capital market cycle.

59   Valuers determine the capital value of commercial property

based on the last rent achieved. Since bank covenants – the security for lending – have to be honoured, there is a natural tendency to keep vacant units in large developments empty rather than offer them at a lower rent: reducing rent for one would bring the capital value of the whole development down. As a result, a game of "Let's pretend" ensues.

60   Also, debt reduces disposable income. Since it is generally the less well-off who borrow, expanding credit makes inequality worse. This is probably why most Western nations show worsening inequality. Economists use a measure called the Gini coefficient, which has been rising: a higher number shows bigger differences in wealth. How paradoxical that in a number of countries, governments of the people have been their oppressors.

61   *Prospect,* Issue 140, November 2007, *How we "count" migration,* Michael Blastland and Andrew Dilnot.

62   The absurd result of a political objective to cap net immigration is that genuine skilled immigration is being curtailed as a result of changes in the inward and outward flow of British nationals.

63   *Council of Mortgage Lenders* press release, 11th November 2010.

64   During the years preceding the credit crunch, mortgage equity withdrawal (now renamed housing equity withdrawal) rose sharply, through increased borrowing secured on existing properties. The Bank of England publish statistics on their website, which show that at the peak, some 8% of after-tax household income was raised in this way. The following table shows the change in secured lending to individuals and money withdrawn from property in the three and a half years from 1st January 2004 to 30th June 2007:

Housing equity withdrawal   £161.4 bn
Increase in total secured lending to individuals £358.0 bn
*Source: Bank of England statistics tables LPQBE92 and LPQVTVJ**

The majority of housing equity withdrawal was obtained through increased borrowing by roughly half of households that had mortgages. Some would have been genuine "last-time sellers" where the proceeds went to savings, but this was partly offset by first-time buyers. Most of the money taken out by extra borrowing must have been spent - and reported as a rise in GDP.

Now let's look at property market transactions. The basic statistics are that, counting by number of transactions, 18% did not involve a mortgage. 82% were mortgaged, consisting of 67% new purchase transactions and 15% remortgage transactions. However, counting by total number of households, 46% of households do not have mortgages - these people mostly stay in the same homes. The activity was driven by borrowing, since 82% of property transactions related to the 54% of households that were mortgaged. Prices were set by the majority of transactions, which only happened because credit was available. Borrowing ruled new home ownership almost as much as it ruled the total market. The growth in the total number of mortgaged properties was roughly the same as the growth in the number of households. The proportion of existing households without mortgages steadily reduced as new households borrowed. [Mortgage data from Council of Mortgage Lenders website, reproduced by permission. Aggregate property data from National Statistics - Contains public sector information licensed under the Open Government Licence v1.0. The derivation is mine.]

While it is not possible to prove conclusively from the figures alone that availability of mortgages fuelled the rise in house prices, the coincidence is remarkable. Is it just coincidence that prices fell when the mortgage supply dried up? Common sense says that availability of easy credit caused house price rises. The extra 'value' in property then became the basis of a self-fulfilling prophecy that prices always rise. This looks remarkably like the sort of perpetual money machine described in histories of the South Sea bubble. The growth in mortgage debt probably helped house prices to rise.

* see *www.bankofengland.co.uk* and also the bank's revisions policy at *www.bankofengland.co.uk/mfsd/iadb/notesiadb/Revisions.htm*

65   Total mortgage debt outstanding was £1,078 bn at end 2006 *(Council of Mortgage Lenders)*.

66   *Sunday Times*, 14th November 2010, *Ireland's sinking feeling*, John Arlidge.

67   Based on data from OECD (2011), "Balance of payments", Main Economic Indicators (database), OECD.Stat Extracts, http://stats.oecd.org , accessed on 6th August 2011.

68   Comparing data internationally is always difficult. There is a standardisation programme in effect for European Union countries, but other OECD countries may not publish entirely comparable data. This standardisation programme has been operative for several years. My original data was taken from the OECD website in 2004 and the 2006 data was added in early 2008. Practices regarding average exchange rates used to translate into US dollars will, inevitably, be inconsistent.

69   My original data was taken from *The Economist*, 24th April 2003. *The Economist* revise their hamburger standard regularly and the latest can be found on their website.

70   The history of how nations emerge from obscurity to become major players on the world stage is that such nations emerge during a period of rapid growth, are hit hard when a crash

comes, and then resume strong growth after the crash. For examples, consider Holland (Tulip mania), England (the South Sea bubble), France (John Law's Mississippi scheme).

71   The carry trade attempts to exploit this by borrowing in a low-yielding currency to invest in a higher-yielding currency, thereby driving expensive currencies to extreme over-valuation.

72   *Baseline Scenario*, 6th April 2010 (www.baselinescenario.com). A complementary argument that bailouts of European countries constitute a Ponzi scheme appeared in the *Financial Times* on 6th May 2011, *Europe is running a giant Ponzi scheme*, Mario Blejer.

73   King Canute showed the noblemen that he had no power to stop the tide coming in.

74   Attempting to ban short selling is a classic own goal. Short sellers add liquidity to markets and enable price discovery, by taking an opposite point of view to the majority. The fashion now is to prevent true price discovery, by restricting or banning short selling and encouraging use of tracker funds. In my view, this is a factor destroying price stability and encouraging crashes.

75   Japan does lead the world in showing how intractable this deflation is.

76   Stein Ringen, *Financial Times* letters, 27th July 2010, *Economists really must ask: what do we know?*

77   The debate was conducted through opposing opinion-editorial pieces in the pages of the *Financial Times* in summer 2010. On one hand, the Keynesians were arguing for continued stimulus and no austerity. Against them were ranged a combination of Ricardians, small state believers (such as the US Republican Tea Party movement) and austere

balance-the-books people (including the present British government, although it is questionable whether the present British government really is balancing the books).

78 *13 Bankers, The Wall Street Takeover and the Next Financial Meltdown,* Simon Johnson and James Kwak, Pantheon 2010.

79 John Kay, *Financial Times,* 17th November 2010, *Bonds designed to leave savers bemused.*

80 Nations always emerge from obscurity by trading in goods, since this can generate a surplus to plough back into growth. Services follow later. Thus, manufacturing is the foundation of prosperity.

81 Economists measure investment in inventories and physical assets, and in GDP terms, manufacturing is represented by investment. However, the word "investment" has been misused by politicians in recent years to mean spending, so I prefer the descriptive term "manufacturing."

82 Before Britain left the Exchange Rate Mechanism in 1992, opinion-formers who dominate the news pages took the conventional line that devaluation would cause inflation. After the event, economists found that spare capacity in the economy had thwarted this relationship.

83 *The Sunday Telegraph,* 19th August 2007, *Boom in quangos costs Britain £170 bn a year,* Robert Watts.

84 Direct government spending on goods and services is around 27% of GDP. Another 23% or so of GDP consists of transfer payments through taxation and benefits. The recipients have a degree of freedom in how they spend this largesse – but some of it is government provided (e.g. certain charges for health care) and discretionary spending is limited by the essential needs of the less well off.

85 For example, police preventing heroism in tragic situations

such as domestic fires, on health and safety grounds (*The Times* news report, 30th March 2009).

86   When people believe they are entitled to something free, demand increases as alternatives are neglected. British society has acquired a culture of entitlements and expectations of free goods and services.

87   Budget 2011, HM Treasury. See note 28 re copyright.

88   The present austerity plan slows the growth in public sector spending, but neither stabilises nor significantly reduces it. Cutting the devotion of private sector resources to public objectives is a quite different project. Actually reversing the resources wasted on compliance would, I believe, enable costs to fall, making Britain more competitive in the world and curtailing some inflation. However, reversing the growth in such overheads would, in the short run, add to the contractionary forces.

89   Twenty years ago, direct costs of tax collection averaged 1.16% of gross tax revenue and direct compliance costs averaged 2.52%, see *Administrative and Compliance Costs of Taxation*, Sandford, Godwin and Hardwick, Fiscal Publications 1989.

90   Nor do leaders learn from history.

91   *Sunday Times*, 5th May 1991, *Lies, damned lies and political statements*, David Smith.

92   *Sunday Times*, 9th February 1992, *Ageing model leads the Treasury astray*, Brian Reading.

93   *The Economist*, 13th June 1992, leading article, *Pick a number*.

94   *Financial Times*, 21st September 1992, letters, *Record shows Treasury never forecast a recession in UK at all*, Prof. Wynne Godley.

95   UK household debt was about £1 trillion in 2006 and £1.5

trillion in July 2008, at which level it represented 173% of average household income. This is believed to be a worldwide record. Official UK government debt is now close to £1 trillion, excluding the hidden debts of the Private Finance Initiative (see notes 27 and 28 above), public sector pensions and sundry other off-balance sheet items. The Centre for Policy Studies published a paper by Brooks Newmark MP, *The Hidden Debt Bombshell*, in 2009, estimating total UK government debt as £2.2 trillion or £85,610 per household, or 158.8% of GDP. Total UK debt has already exceeded the limit described by Reinhardt and Rogoff (see note 7 above). It is the combination of both public and private debt that is so severe in Britain.

96   Chapter 4 gave some examples.

97   According to Dr Hugo Bänziger (*Financial Times*, 27th April 2010, *Basel rules must address shortfalls of the past*), the forthcoming new Basel rules for bank capital requirements will prompt every bank to raise capital or reduce lending at the same time when the cycle next turns, by imposing complete uniformity of requirements instead of allowing diversity. In my view, bigger crises are the inevitable result of imposing ever increasing regulation. This is the essence of the case for returning to evolutionary finance.

98   *Psychology of Crowds (Psychologie des Foules)*, Gustave le Bon, republished by Sparkling Books (ISBN 978-1-907230-08-0)

99   Writing off debt means there must be credit losses as well. Somebody has to pay for the losses. This is the underlying problem with all schemes to recapitalise failing banks, as with schemes to compensate lost deposits by making others pay. It also applies to proposals to restructure debt, for example in the Euro zone (*The Economist*, 14th January 2011, *Bite the bullet*). Who will take the losses? Those promoting restruct-

uring overlook this.

100 I found 192 UN members plus Vatican City, excluding Taiwan, Kosovo and South Sudan.

101 The financial establishment likes to argue differently, that if there are fewer younger people then the value of savings must rise. See also my comments on supply and demand arguments under "Government bond markets" in chapter 5. Arguments and advice based on static comparisons at one moment in time rarely allow for future trend changes or the changing dynamics of the world.

102 *The Wisdom of Crowds*, James Surowiecki, Little, Brown Book Group 2004.

103 *Flat Earth News*, Nick Davies, Chatto & Windus 2008.

104 This is, in effect, what the money markets achieved with the credit crunch.

105 In early 2008, I found a "rare opportunity to acquire a mobile phone mast" advertised on an estate agent's website.

106 This was deliberate. The bureaucracy argued at the time that being obliged to consider competition might have restricted their ability to enforce rules. This is not the same as the light touch régime in wholesale markets.

107 *The Times*, 10th December 2009, *Act smart: don't burn quangos, reform them*, Prof. Matthew Flinders.

108 There are some honourable exceptions, such as the Financial Services Authority's demand for banks to stress test extreme downturns. My concern is that judgment and anticipation are so lacking.

109 Skills are only brought into the House of Commons by a change of government, since a proportion of newly-elected Members will have followed other careers than politics and there are few by-elections. Outside skills are in decline as

cradle-to-grave politicians replace broadly educated men and women with experience in other walks of life.

110   *Does Britain need a Financial Regulator?* Philip Booth and Terry Arthur, Institute of Economic Affairs, 2010.

111   *The Human Side of Enterprise,* Douglas McGregor, The McGraw Hill Companies, Inc. 1960.

112   To be turned into an employee owned mutual, competing with the established auditors (*Financial Times,* 4th April 2011, *Audit agency prepares for mutual future,* Jim Pickard).

113   *Local Government Chronicle,* 16th July 2009. See also *Systems Thinking in the Public Sector: the failure of the reform régime... and a manifesto for a better way,* John Seddon, Triarchy Press 2008.

114   Dan Waters, FSA Director of Retail Policy & Conduct Risk, http://www.fsa.gov.uk/pages/Library/Communication/Speech es/2009/0116_dw.shtml 16th January 2009 © The Financial Services Authority 2009.

115   The Securities and Exchange Commission presumes that accounts which do not comply with standards are misleading or inaccurate (D. R. Myddelton, *Financial Times* letters 22nd December 2009, *Accounting stifles freedom of thought*). Until 2009, UK law presumed that accounts which complied with standards "however unreliable, imprudent and lacking economic substance" were deemed to be true and fair (Stella Fearnley, *Financial Times* letters 22nd December 2009, *A long history of being stupid*).

116   The particular faults with International Financial Reporting Standards were described by Timothy Bush, *Financial Times* letters, 29th December 2009, *Accounting takes over from regulation as the prime suspect.*

117   *The Economist,* Leading article *What went wrong with economics,* and Briefing, *The state of economics,* 18th July 2009.

118 Bootle lists nine egregious fallacies that, in his experience, financial advisers frequently fall for. I particularly like his reference to the belief that everyone can make money out of financial speculation (which is impossible), his description of equity returns as akin to an Indian rope trick and the thought that financial advisers are too often ignorant of history. *The Trouble with Markets: Saving Capitalism from Itself*, Roger Bootle, Nicholas Brealey Publishing 2009, pp 173-4.

119 My comments on the failings of the economics profession are mild compared to Bootle's (Op cit pp 21 ff).

120 Keynes thought booms should be moderated before they got out of hand.

121 Rod Dowler, *Financial Times* letters, 12th August 2010, *Let a physicist take charge of economics*.

122 Any fluctuations in price should follow a bell shaped pattern, the majority of price observations closely grouped around the mean, with a very small chance of extreme variations.

123 Joseph Stiglitz, *Financial Times*, 20th August 2010, *Needed, a new economic paradigm*.

124 The price paid for a fixed interest stock is expressed as a percentage of maturity value. The coupon of a fixed interest stock is the rate of interest as a percentage of the maturity value. Thus a purchase at 100 will result in income at the same rate as the coupon. A purchase above 100 will result in a capital loss if the stock is held to maturity and income below the coupon. A purchase below 100 will result in income above the coupon and a capital gain if the stock is held to maturity. High coupon stocks issued many years ago, when interest rates were higher, will usually trade at prices above 100. It is often said that prices and income move in opposite directions, but once you have bought a fixed interest stock, the income

you earn is fixed: only new buyers notice the change. In a deflationary era in which rates tend ever lower, high quality fixed interest stocks (i.e. government bonds) provide a means to project high yields forward for thirty years or more. Even though short-term rates are close to zero, long-term rates have further to fall and will do so if inflation turns into deflation.

125 In the United Kingdom, index linked Gilts have their repayment value at maturity and interest coupons adjusted in line with inflation. The income adjustment is less than a casual observer might expect, since if inflation is 3% the coupon is simply multiplied by 1.03. There is a catch: the indexing formula works downwards as well as upwards, so if inflation gives way to deflation, index linked Gilts will bring losses in both capital and income.

126 With private investors often buying last in the rise and selling last in the fall. A Mr Alastair Lennox from Leicester said on BBC Money Box, 6th August 2005, repeated 8th August : ".. like all small shareholders we tend to get in at the top and out at the bottom. I just hope I'm not being brought into buying shares again, finding that it's peaked and on its way down." *(programme transcript)*

127 The converse is also true: people who do not sell at 20% or 30% losses, decide to sell out at 80% or 90% losses.

128 "Gilts – do you really need them?" Sara Webb, *Financial Times*, 14th April 1990.

129 Only Imperial Tobacco appears in both the 1958 FT 30 index and the 2008 FTSE 100 index. For part of the time, it was a subsidiary of Hanson.

130 In the Dow Jones index.

131 Except when something goes awry, such as BP's accident that led to a dividend cut and share price fall.

132 The hardest part is to sell into a rally. This is when the newspapers start to announce a glorious future for equities, quoting City sources. In bear markets, the rallies do not last, but they do outlast the daily news cycle.

133 See, for example, *Fault Lines: How Hidden Fractures Still Threaten the World Economy*, Raghuram G. Rajan, © Princeton University Press 2010. Arguments that global growth will continue also appear regularly in opinion-editorial columns.

134 *The Collapse of Complex Societies*, J. A. Tainter, Cambridge University Press 1989.

135 Nassim Nicholas Taleb and Mark Spitznagel, *Financial Times*, July 14th 2009, *Time to tackle the real evil: too much debt.*

Further reading

Inclusion in this list does not signify that the author of this work agrees with the arguments made. Please see the footnote given for the full reference.

Index

Sparkling Books

Imaginations

Sally Speding, *Malediction*

David Stuart Davies, *Brothers in Blood*

Luke Hollands, *Peregrine Harker and the Black Death*

Sally Spedding, *Cold Remains*

Tony Bayliss, *Past Continuous*

Brian Conaghan, *The Boy Who Made it Rain*

Anna Cuffaro, *Gatwick Bear and the Secret Plans*

Nikki Dudley, *Ellipsis*

Alan Hamilton, *Two Unknown*

Amanda Sington-Williams, *The Eloquence of Desire*

Perspectives

Daniele Cuffaro, *American Myths in Post-9/11 Music*

Revivals

Carlo Goldoni, *Il vero amico / The True Friend*

Gustave Le Bon, *Psychology of Crowds*

For further Revivals and more information visit:

www.sparklingbooks.com

Sparkling Books